THE
LIVELY
SCIENCE

D1500693

R. Shaun Maloney

THE LIVELY SCIENCE

REMODELING HUMAN SOCIAL RESEARCH

MICHAEL AGAR

MILL CITY PRESS, MINNEAPOLIS

Copyright © 2013 by Michael Agar.
www.ethknoworks.com

Mill City Press, Inc.
212 3rd Avenue North, Suite 290
Minneapolis, MN 55401
612.455.2294
www.millcitypublishing.com

All rights reserved. No part of this publication may be reproduced, stored in a retrieval system, or transmitted, in any form or by any means, electronic, mechanical, photocopying, recording, or otherwise, without the prior written permission of the author.

ISBN-13: 978-1-62652-102-5
LCCN: 2013905921

Book Design by Mary Kristin Ross

Printed in the United States of America

TABLE OF CONTENTS

PREFACE

Getting in a Book Mood

What's a nice reader like you doing in a book like this? I'm hoping that you're here because you're curious about a way to do "behavioral science" or "social science" that will help you figure out a problem you'd like to solve, or maybe you just wonder what those words mean because you're a curious type. Maybe you're a student, new or returning, embarking on a course with those names attached to it, or maybe a course in one of the many other areas that make use of them.

The point is, I'm writing for readers who are fresh to the concepts, not for colleagues. This book has a simple premise to get you started. The premise is, *research on humans in their social world by other humans is not a traditional science like the one created by Galileo and Newton.* It's not that the creators were wrong. Far from it. The ones who were wrong were the historical figures who tried to imitate the way the creators worked, neglecting the fact that learning how people make it through the day is different from dropping balls from the Leaning Tower of Pisa or getting hit on the head by falling apples. Galileo didn't have to communicate with the balls. Besides, he didn't have to worry that the balls might look down 185 feet and refuse to jump and throw him over the parapet instead.

All sciences make their case based on evidence according to the rules of some logic, and then they try and prove the case wrong in order to show that it might be right. But once a human makes other humans in their social world the scientific focus, all sorts of problems come up that didn't appear with material objects or with most non-human forms of life. True, the problems start to show up the closer the animal gets to Homo sapiens. Chimpanzees, it turns out, are a lot harder to research than ants, and humans are even more complicated than chimps.

It's an old argument, a couple of centuries old now, that human social science is a different breed of scientific cat, but this is *not* a book with broad and deep coverage of that history. I'll use that long history as a conclusion, as the basis for a "lively science," not as a debate to be re-hashed yet again. This book will use a few key figures and a few key concepts to outline why a human social science is different and then take it from there. The fact that it's different does not mean it isn't a science. It does mean that it has to be done differently than an experiment in a chemistry lab.

The Lively Science is about how to form a question and think of ways to answer it in a different scientific way. The hundred-dollar word is *epistemology*. It's not a common word used around the house, as Groucho Marx used to say on his classic TV show, *You Bet Your Life*, but it is a straightforward word that means the nature of knowledge and how it is acquired. The problem the book zeroes in on is simply this: The behavioral and social sciences adopted the *wrong* epistemology. But then what does the *right* epistemology look like? That's the question I want to answer here.

Mostly this book is driven by experiences during the last 15 years or so, starting with the day I left the university to work on a variety of different projects in the so-called "real world," a place I have tried to locate for years without success. Several of those projects will be used as examples. Their variety, and the people I worked with, taught me to think and speak in a more general way about an alternative human social science. That alternative was why people sought me out, because the traditional way of doing human social science had cost them a lot of money and produced little in the way of useful results. Thanks to them, I got better and better at describing the alternative, how it was different, and what it could and, even more importantly, could not do. This book is a summary of what I learned to say to them, together with a selective look back at history to find out that what I was learning had, as usual, already been said by many people a long time ago.

A note about notes before we start: The book rests on a few key references, many of which are mentioned in the text itself. Chapter notes at the end will give other citations and a few suggestions for additional reading should anyone want to dive into deeper waters. Those who would like to join the professional club have some investment of time and energy ahead of them, but anyone who makes it through this book should have a general sense of how "the lively science" works.

My thanks to the many colleagues and students over the decades, inside and outside the halls of academe, for the conversations and questions and answers that helped shape this book. Thanks also to the State of Maryland for the partial pension after 16 years of work as a professor and to the Social Security Administration for the monthly check. Between the two of them they provided enough money so I could carve out time from my current self-employed life to write this book. Most of my thanks go to Ellen Taylor, mi vieja, as they say with affection in New Mexico, who not only tolerated this project but also generously helped to shape it.

The mistakes, as the saying goes, are all mine, but I tried to make them interesting.

CHAPTER ONE

Behavioral/Social Science—An Oxymoron?

In late 2010 the American Anthropological Association considered revising their mission statement to eliminate the word "science." Earlier that same year, Republicans in the House of Representatives had introduced legislation to eliminate funding for "behavioral and social sciences" at the National Science Foundation because they are "often more controversial and less directly related to NSF's core mission." It might be the first time that the AAA and the Republican Party have ever agreed on anything. Anthropology is uncomfortable being called a "science," and the Republicans are uncomfortable including it or any of its behavioral and social science kin in a national "science" foundation.

What is the problem here with using "human," "social" and "science" in the same sentence?

It's not news, this problem. There are the old stories, like the one about President Harry Truman, who told the press he wanted a "one handed economist." When you asked them a question, he said, they always replied, "On the one hand this, on the other hand that." Economists, they say, are the most scientific of the human research lot, but then again, they're the ones that inspired Thomas Carlyle to add the adjective "dismal." The general sentiment was well expressed in the famous line from the poet W.H. Auden, "Thou shalt not sit with statisticians nor commit a social science." Then there are Mark Twain's three kinds of lies, the regular kind, but then "damn lies" and, worst of all, "statistics."

There are older stories still. Goethe wondered how Newton could claim that the spectrum said all there was to say about human perception of color, and Hegel wrote about history, about how time was a dimension of the human situation that the second law of thermodynamics couldn't handle. Some say we can even go further back, to Protagoras, famous for his saying that "man is the measure of all things." He is credited with being the first Sophist, a movement whose reputation only fed the conflict between the appreciation of human social situations, on the one hand, and the for-hire manipulation of words absent any commitment to truth on the other.

None of this inspires a great deal of confidence in human social science, neither in the accuracy of what it has learned, nor in its possible uses. And it all started out on such a positive note, too—literally a "positivistic" one. It began with the optimism born of Newton's discoveries. As Alexander Pope's epitaph for his tomb in Westminster Abbey concluded, "God said let Newton be, and all was light." If all the light was in classical physics, who but a disreputable sleaze would hang out in the dark? The rush was on to make human social science as Newton-like as possible.

August Comte, whom many would consider the founder of sociology in the early 19th century, called his work "social physics" to honor the master. His "positivism" was a sociology that included the preceding tradition of physical science—empirical, quantitative, guided by hypothesis-testing experiments. Positivism, he argued, would solve the social problems of post-revolutionary France. That didn't work out so well either.

Human social science has always been a problem child. In the eyes of those outside the profession, the famous—and often inaccurate—quote sometimes comes to mind, that human social science is "the painful elaboration of the obvious." Worse is the phrase of those who shift their gaze from some new technological marvel from Silicon Valley to the results of a social survey, that the whole enterprise is "pseudo-science." And within the professional human social research world, a clear caste system ranks its members. Experimental methods and mathematical equations are at the top; the words and actions of people in their everyday lives are at the bottom.

This ranking is a two hundred-year-old mistake. That is the first premise of this book. The second premise is that the mistake occurred because human social science tried to be the wrong kind of science. The third premise is that a different kind of science has been waiting in the wings for a couple of centuries, and it's high time to move it from the margins to the center, because it grounds human social science in what it is supposed to be about – us, in our everyday lives, for better or for worse, 'til death do us part. And the fourth and final premise: None of this excludes traditional science; it includes it as one character, though not the author, in a much larger story of how humans describe and explain other humans in a scientific mode.

"Data" for a science is a construction born of an interaction between scientist and world. This is 20th Century physics, not some tagline from an obsolete postmodern theory. The problem for human social science is that it usually tries to construct data in a way that imitates as closely as possible a traditional science laboratory. What that boils down to is a simplified situation isolated from real life that usually doesn't resemble it at all, designed and controlled by a scientist. The problem is that, most of the time, those kinds of situations are *not* the phenomena that the science, in the end, wants to describe or explain.

Our lives are seldom like the experimental frameworks that the scientists shoehorn us into. We can't be described and explained absent some sense of our beliefs, feelings, desires, and purposes. Outside the research setting, we live in social webs that influence what we think and do, as in the famous "theorem" (a bad metaphor if ever there was one) of W.I. Thomas in 1928, that if people define a social situation as real, it is real in its consequences.

There are other ways to get the science job done with all the critical steps, namely, *evidence organized by logic to reach a conclusion that is then tested by trying to prove it wrong.* The historical problem is, those other ways look chaotic if not psychotic from a traditional point of view. They are not. The problem, the one this book will try to solve, is how to make an alternative way of doing science clear so that an interested reader can get a sense of how it works and how to evaluate its results.

A recent historical wave aimed to do exactly that, a wave usually called *qualitative research.* There is in fact a link between the two hundred year old history of an alternative human social science—the foundation on which this book rests—and the more recent qualitative story. But the exponential explosion of the "qualitative" field and the promiscuous use of the term have muddied it considerably. Comte-like positivists use propositional data and call their research "qualitative" now. Some "qualitative" researchers do projects that have nothing in common with the concept of "science" used in this book.

The only clear meaning of "qualitative" versus "quantitative" at this point is data consisting of "propositions" as opposed to data consisting of "numbers." But an alternative to Comte isn't about what data a researcher *should* use. It is about research that assumes a researcher will use numbers, propositions, and any other kind of information she can find that will help learn more about a particular human social world. It's not numbers versus propositions. It's how both of them, and other kinds of information as well, are gathered and put together in a different way. It's about epistemology.

Human Social Science?

"Human social science" is an odd-looking phrase that is one of three that will occur so often in this book that it would be good to talk about them now. The reason for "human" and "social" is this: *The two terms label different levels of organization—person and group.* You can see the split in most traditional disciplines— micro- and macro-economics for example, or in the academic labels that signal both levels at the same time, like psychological anthropology or social psychology.

I'll deal with this two-level problem later. For the moment, this book will worry about any kind of science where both researcher and "object" of study are human "subjects," whether with a focus on the individual or on the group or on both. They will all be lumped together as *human social science.*

There is yet another level, the biological, and another set of terms that blur the levels, like "sociobiology" and "biocultural" and "cognitive neuroscience." Here and there in the book that lower organizational level will come into play. By and large, though, the focus here will be on *individual* humans in their *social* world, *as they experience it and act in it.* And the argument in this book will be that those levels are where the descriptions and expla- nations of a human social science must originate and return to at the end of the day.

The next two phrases will be used so frequently that I am going to turn them into acronyms. First, some background. The mainstream tradition that came out of the Newtonian era is often called the "received view." It is called that because it is like a caught pass in football with nothing left to do but to run for the goal. The core premise of the received view is that any science, whatever its focus, is at base the same. So what is science? Here is what my New Oxford American computer dictionary says it means:

> ...the intellectual and practical activity encompassing the systematic study of the structure and behavior of the physical and natural world through observation and experiment.

Notice there's not a lot of human and social in there. But never mind. Let's take that definition and see what it turned into in human social science.

This received view is often called "behavioral and social science." The phrase is a common one. It has been around for decades. I'll give it an acronym for ease of reference in the rest of this book. Let's call it *BSS* for short.

Don't look at me. I didn't invent the phrase that "BSS" is based on. In fact, at the University of Maryland they called the administrative unit that includes the human and social sciences "BSOS." You can imagine the irreverent comments from my colleagues in the so-called "hard" sciences—to use the usual phallic metaphor—not to mention others in business and engineering. The "OS" was sometimes interpreted as "out of sight," and, with time, as "operating system." The "BS" part you can guess.

BSS, in an oversimplified nutshell, is Enlightenment science carried forward into human social realms. It marches to the tune of the "experimental method," as outlined by John Stuart Mill in *A System of Logic* in 1843. I'm going to talk about him at length in the next chapter. So prestigious is this method in the world of science, so often is it held up as the Holy Grail, that research centers like the National Institutes of Health call it "the gold standard," as do many other places. They still do, in spite of the fact that President Nixon abandoned the real gold standard in 1971. If not a dead metaphor, it's at least deep-frozen.

Here's a stripped-down version of how science converts human social behavior into scientific gold. Real examples are of course more complicated than this sketch, but I think most mavens would agree that what is to come catches the heart of it, or at least some of its vital organs.

First, imagine a statement that you want to test scientifically. Where does the statement come from? It is deduced from a theory, a generalization about how things are. In human social science, the theory is usually in ordinary language. The statement is called a *hypothesis*. A hypothesis must be true, or at least not wrong, if the theory is true.

A scientist wants to try and *falsify* the hypothesis, in other words, prove it wrong, just like the philosopher Karl Popper said science must try and do. If it isn't falsified, then the theory still stands. Notice that a hypothesis, and therefore a theory, is never *proven* in any simple way, not according to Popper. They just keep surviving test after test, or not, as the case may be. This version of "proof" is hotly debated these days, but that is more than we need to deal with right now.

How do you try and prove it wrong? This is where the founders of science revolutionized history. "Proof" in the Middle Ages meant, check it against the papal authorities in Rome or the Aristotelian scholars in the university. No more, said the new scientists. Let's take a first-hand look at what the world is actually doing instead of looking it up in Aristotle or the Bible to see if what we say is true corresponds to what is already believed. This new revolutionary plan for testing ideas was called *empirical*, or "verifiable by observation or experience."

So began a conflict between those who look to the world for information and those who preach how the world must be because they think it is so in the privacy of their own minds. The conflict is as current as today's headlines. An early famous case was Galileo, who said that, given all the observations that had been made, the sun, not the earth, had to be at the center of the universe. After his trial by the Inquisition he spent the rest of his life under house arrest, the advantage there being that he got a lot of writing done.

Science has to be *empirical* and *falsifiable*. All science, human/social or any other. In this sense, all science *is* the same.

But is that enough? What if you don't have a theory or a hypothesis? What if you just want to explore how the world works? When they asked Einstein how he came up with the theory of relativity, he said he imagined what it would be like to ride around on a beam of light. Was that a hypothesis? He sounds like a Grateful Dead fan. And he was just dealing with particles. What if the particles had their own ideas of what they were doing and he had to first learn and later explain that? He'd have to get to know them and their true inner feelings. Would that have been a hypothesis? The notion of real science as just testing a hypothesis doesn't describe its most creative moments. BSS tends to leave that creative part of the story out of its final reports.

After the hypothesis has been concocted, a researcher has to figure out a way to *measure* the *variables*, the variables being the things that vary in the hypothesis. Measurement means figuring out a way to assign a number to the variables that represents their magnitude. One of the variables is called "dependent." It is the one to be explained by the other variable, which is called "independent."

Real science has to be based on numbers. The law of gravity wasn't a song or a punch line to a joke; it was an equation. As Galileo said:

> Philosophy is written in this grand book — I mean the universe — which stands continually open to our gaze, but it cannot be understood unless one first learns to comprehend the language and interpret the characters in which it is written. It is written in the language of mathematics, and its characters are triangles, circles, and other geometrical figures, without which it is humanly impossible to understand a single word of it; without these, one is wandering around in a dark labyrinth.

Never mind that Galileo speaks of mathematics and geometry, not measurement and statistics. Never mind another famous Einstein quote, that not everything that counts can be counted and that not everything that can be counted counts. Sometimes numbers are, in fact, the right language. But the rule that numbers are the *only* possible language for science is nonsense. My friend and colleague, Steve Banks, was a mathematics Ph.D. He used to give me a hard time. He'd say, "You tell people they either deal with numbers or propositions? I wrote a math dissertation that didn't have much of either of those two things in it. So what am I, chopped liver?"

BSS bought into this number-centric epistemology and ran with it. To get the kind of controlled quantitative data that the laboratory fantasy required, it simplified and controlled and reduced, usually into something that resembled nothing that research subjects would ordinarily do. Subject worlds were only allowed into the research as permitted by a narrow design of the scientist's own making. What happened in BSS research and what happened in life usually didn't have much to do with each other.

BSS results are usually boring to everyone but colleagues who are disciplinary insiders. It had better be interesting to them, because they are the ones who—through "peer review"—control access to grants, journals and promotion and tenure in the traditional academic world. Their version of science makes BSS look more like a laboratory, but less like the human social world it claims to be about. That is the fundamental flaw in this epistemological story that needs to be fixed —not by abolishing BSS, but by reducing it from a gold standard to just another currency for use in the market of those who strive to learn how the human social world does and does not work in a scientific way.

The Fork in the Road

When the received view of science expanded into the human and the social, it turned "human social science" into BSS and little else. BSS grew into the statistical test of quantitative hypotheses derived from prior theory. Data for the test relied on "instruments" or experimental "manipulations," or to available aggregate databases, with little if any question about the way a phenomenon of interest actually took shape in the lives of research subjects, or whether the phenomenon had any correspondence to anything in those lives at all. The research results might have made the hearts of colleagues soar like an eagle. But I always imagine the subjects, or those research consumers who were interested in learning more about them, wondering what the researchers had smoked for breakfast.

"Received view" human social science became a rule that the *only* way a scientist could do research would be to strap a project into a BSS straitjacket. It was like telling someone that the only tool they could use to build a house was a caulking gun. It's a useful tool, but extremely limited in what it can do, and a poor choice for most of what needs to be done besides caulking, especially if you forgot to bring the tube of caulk.

I need one more acronym in addition to BSS before I start the book, one that can refer to an alternative kind of human social science, the "lively science" as I call it here. It has had many names, not all of them suitable for a family book of this type. Dilthey, discussed in Chapter Three, called it "Geisteswissenschaft," but that's hard for English speakers to dance to. I'll call it, simply enough, "human social research," and I'll refer to it with the acronym *HSR*.

So there's behavioral social science or BSS, and human social research or HSR, both of which are kinds of human social science. I'm going to set BSS and HSR up as separate but unequal ways to do human social science in the first part of the book. As the story moves along, they will start to talk with each other. The book will evolve to show that HSR is the more general framework that can include BSS. But without HSR we can't know why a question is important or whether its answer explains anything. At the end of the book, I'm going to challenge the "separate but unequal" argument with one of the most famous BSS studies of all times, one I admire— Stanley Milgram's experiments where ordinary people jolted each other with doses of electricity because a guy in a white coat in a science lab told them to. Milgram was a genius, but by the end of the book it will be obvious that his "experiment" was actually a BSS moment in a broad and deep HSR context.

To begin the book, though, I'll start by foregrounding the

differences. I'll start with a few 19th century thinkers. They argued over whether or not one human researching some other humans was a different kind of science, and they left a treasure trove of ideas for how to develop an alternative. Their ideas didn't die. On the contrary, they survived on marginal academic and practical islands right up until the present.

Some BSS types use the obsolete word "postmodern" for any criticism of their traditional monopoly. That is not what is in play here. Some HSR types, in turn, call BSS the perfect example of "scientism," with all the connotations of racism, sexism, and classism lumbering along in the semantic background. Not in this book. But the argument that human social science isn't your grandfather's chemistry set makes perfect sense, and that is the starting point for now.

A Trailer for the Movie

As a preview of the book, consider some of the ways that HSR will be different from BSS, given the sketch of how traditional science works.

1. With BSS, a hypothesis is framed *before* the research starts and it can't change. In HSR a hypothesis changes as more is learned during a project, and new ones will appear and be considered well *after* the project starts.

2. A BSS hypothesis is made up of "independent" and "dependent" variables. In HSR there aren't any independent variables. There are, however, patterns that link variables together in many different ways, including feedback loops that undermine many statistical techniques.

3. Where does a BSS hypothesis come from? Usually from a single academic theory. HSR will probably use several theories to formulate research questions and then make up a few more as the case requires and as more is learned during a project. BSS is theory testing; HSR is also theory-generating.

4. BSS is empirical, maybe observational, like the earlier definition of "science" requires, but only within the limits of an interview or experiment or aggregate dataset designed and controlled by a researcher. HSR is open to information from any source, researcher designed or not.

5. The BSS model requires assumptions like *standardization*—every subject sees the interview/experiment in exactly the same way—and *ceteris parabus*—nothing varies *systematically* except the variables in the hypothesis. HSR, in contrast, accepts that neither assumption is ever true in any human social world.

6. To convert a human moment into a number, BSS assumes the number means something that it doesn't necessarily mean to research subjects. HSR focuses more on discovering patterns that mean something to subjects rather than numerical measurements of variables.

7. Both BSS and HSR worry about sampling, but BSS designs a sample before a project starts and HSR modifies it during a project as more is learned about variation among subjects that matter given a particular research question.

8. Most statistics include prior assumptions about the variables, the samples and the population that BSS usually doesn't investigate. In fact, popular statistical software, last time I looked, didn't make it easy to examine a raw distribution of data. Worse, some statistics assume a normal distribution when in fact the variable of interest may well be distributed in many other ways. In HSR a frequent non-normal distribution is that a few patterns occur a lot and a few others are rare, something popularized recently as the "black swan" effect, also called by the unflattering name of "fat tails."

9. In BSS, assumptions about research subjects are often made to fit a theory's premises. Consider the classic economics assumption, that an economic actor is a rational agent free of social influence making decisions on the basis of perfect information. Imagine an obsessively greedy Spock-like figure checking the Dow on the Enterprise computer. HSR modifies assumptions about subjects and their worlds based on what is learned from them. HSR subjects are more complicated and life-like in research reports than BSS subjects are.

10. BSS aspires to a goal of *objectivity*, the notion that the researcher and his or her biographical and historical context have no influence on the research. HSR rejects this goal as delusional when humans research other humans. HSR science is, at its base, *intersubjective*, neither "objective" nor "subjective" in any simple way.

As I said, this is only meant as a preview, and, hopefully, it raises a lot of interesting questions for the reader. Notice how most everything on the HSR side of the comparison describes characteristics that the BSS received view would describe as "unscientific." The argument in this book is that these characteristics are not unscientific; they are signals that a *different* kind of science is in motion, a science that adapts to the realities of a research done by a human that is about humans, but one that retains characteristics of science like falsification, evidence based on empirical data, logic, and systematic presentation of results.

HSR Ascendant in the Real World

As I write this, in 2012, I make a living in part by working on projects driven by a popular interest in more, rather than less, HSR type science. Where does this "real world" interest come from?

The harsh and arguable answer is, BSS just hasn't helped much when it comes to understanding and acting on problems in actual human social worlds. Yet many human social scientists, from the founders described in the next two chapters to the present, have announced the noble goal of doing exactly that. All of that positive Enlightenment promise, now viewed through the rearview mirror—all that positivism with which Comte jump-started sociology to make post-revolutionary France age like smooth Bordeaux. Was it all just smoke and mirrors?

This collapse of Enlightenment optimism in human social science left us with President Truman's joke and Auden's line of poetry mentioned at the start of this chapter. But then comes what feels like a new era, things pick up again, not heading for a happy ending like a Hollywood movie, but an ending that shows the "arc of character." The protagonists learn from the crisis and become more comfortable with their limits, getting on with life in a less naïve but more accepting way.

I think this is what's happening today with human social science. I've seen the change in my own lifetime, now into what I learned to call "the third age" in Spanish, namely, when you get past sixty. I started out, in the "first age" as a cultural anthropology major in the 1960s. The Vietnam War landed me in a hospital for the treatment of heroin addicts – as a researcher, not as an addict. The most polite question from other researchers and practitioners and administrators at the time was, "How is what you do different from journalism?" They meant, "What you do obviously isn't *science*, so what in the hell is it?" And "journalism" was often prefaced with the qualifier "mere." The irony, at the time, was that the same skeptics were cheering on Woodward and Bernstein as they uncovered the Nixon-era Watergate Scandal.

Times have changed. Now I hear from groups who start by telling me, "We tried science and science didn't work." (They mean BSS.) "We need a better way of figuring out the human social part of the problem we're interested in."

Here's a recent example. An outpatient chemotherapy clinic cares about their patients and wants to reduce the average amount of time they have to spend in the waiting room. They try statistical analysis of records, surveys, time and motion studies, computer models, god knows what else. The results? They could only shave a few minutes off of several hours of waiting time.

They ask me for help. I hang around, listen to patients and front line staff, read a lot of things, and do the kind of "unscientific" looking human social research that this book will be about. It turns out that maybe reducing waiting time is impossible. But patients have different ways of looking at waiting time with a common thread. The thread is *uncertainty*—how much better things go if you know *why* you are waiting, both in terms of what's going on with the clinic and what's going on with your disease. So we plan a system to address that.

Even though not much can be done about the number of minutes, a lot can be done about reducing the uncertainty of those minutes. Even if it's bad news, which it usually isn't on a day-to-day basis, it's better to know one way or the other rather than to assume your cancer just jumped a stage when the real explanation is that a subway delay or another patient's morning test results messed up scheduling. The big chiefs and the patients like the plan. It's almost a happy ending, given that stories about cancer tend not to have one, but then the chiefs shift their priorities to hospital-borne diseases, so the plan goes on the shelf. But still, the case makes the point.

The point is that human social science is more accurate and useful if we stop pretending that it can only occur along the guidelines of a laboratory science. No more pretending that you control all the variables when you're not sure what the most important ones might be. No more talking to someone and ignoring the fact that they hear something different from what you intended and vice-versa. The most important thing learned in human social science is probably going to be a pattern rather than a number, a pattern that a researcher didn't know existed until he was well into a project. The best way to show an audience what was learned will probably be a metaphor rather than an equation. And, most important of all, the way a researcher learns will be in fits and starts, the learning filled with surprises and new concepts that appear in unplanned ways well after the research begins, such that the research itself has to be adjusted and modified as needed.

This HSR alternative, at the end of the day, will still be

systematic, guided by evidence, logic and falsification, just like any science. But it will *never* resemble a carefully scripted step-by-step laboratory experiment. HSR will be more about getting the job done rather than how to do it in micro-managed detail.

Human social research, HSR, is a *different kind of science*. Good human social science of any kind can include numbers, surveys, and indicators. And during the purest HSR study, moments will come that call on the purest of BSS experimental logic, as we'll see in the next chapter. Human social science can, and often must, include these things, but in the end it has to grow from and then re-connect with a more comprehensive investigation of the human social world. Otherwise, what is the science about?

Read a report of traditional human social science and nine times out of ten the most interesting part will be in the "discussion" or "interpretation" section, a section at the end based on the imagination of the researcher. At times it is well done and rings true and makes sense out of a mind-numbing sequence of tables and charts. The material in that section, the material that can make sense out of the research in terms of how the human social world actually works, is the part that needs to be at the center of human social science, not a creative writing task tacked on at the end.

It drives me crazy, even though I've done it myself, when a group of people involved in decision-making cite all kinds of BSS data, but then the pivotal moment that tips the decision one way or another centers on a story about what the neighbor said yesterday or a documentary viewed in the hotel room the night before or a theory the taxi driver presented on the way in from the airport. No disrespect to taxi-drivers. This is terrible human social science used in dangerously important ways. There's no excuse for not doing it right.

"Data" linked to real human social worlds is where human social science, whatever else it does, has to start and has to finish, as long as it wants to claim that in the end human social worlds are what the science is about. The way to fix BSS tunnel vision is, step one, realize that there is a different kind of science, and, step two, make it clear how it works. That's what this book, *The Lively Science,* is all about.

Where Book Titles Come From

The kind of human social science I want to describe here is best understood as a *way of learning, specifically designed for a human interested in figuring out how some others live their lives, followed by a systematic presentation of the results that can be evaluated and challenged.*

The main title of this book is *The Lively Science.* It's a play on the opposite of the "dismal science," as Carlyle called economics back in the 19th century, a century I'm going to dive into for the next two chapters. Supposedly he was inspired to call it "dismal" after reading Malthus' cheery forecast that population growth would outstrip food production and we'd all starve. A different phrase in those days was "the gay science," "die fröhliche Wissenschaft" in the German title of Nietzsche's 1882 book. Another translation into English was "the joyous wisdom." In 2013 "gay" is most frequently used to mean a sexual orientation and "joyous" sounds like a Christmas card, so "lively" seems like a better wording, since the point of this book is that human social science has neglected its phenomenon of interest, namely, human lives in their ordinary social context.

The subtitle of this book, "Remodeling Human Social Research," is written with tongue firmly epoxied in cheek. But the subtitle does convey two serious messages. Here is the first. Many – many – have written about HSR in one form or another over the decades. I'm neglecting a thorough review of that work for the most part and trying to write an accessible and freestanding overview of a way of thinking about human social science. I hope what I've added here is a clearer description of *why* HSR makes sense with a discussion of the epistemology that describes a general view of the *how*. I owe my ability to write this to the many projects I've worked on and workshops I've given for people who asked me about what I do and how they can evaluate the results. Those conversations taught me how to describe HSR in succinct ways. I'm grateful to all those project colleagues over the years who asked sharp questions and demanded clear answers.

The second serious message in the subtitle: This is an informally written book, like a group of independent contractors remodeling a house, with music playing and story- telling and the occasional politically incorrect joke. In my old age I tell people that, because of how I grew up, I think of myself as a craftsman, only I work with ideas rather than materials. The book is written more as a conversation with a reader while working on a job rather than as a piece of scholarly writing. There are contractions and jokes and popular culture references and personal experiences. Some of them are dated, like the author. As you can see in the chapter notes at the end, the book is lightly referenced, in part because some mentions are well-known and easily found, in part because the focus is on a few key representative figures rather than an exhaustive exploration of all who have ever mentioned a topic. Not a style for all readers, I know, but a style that I hope makes a long history of complicated thinking accessible, useful and interesting to those who are curious about a different way to do human social science.

So *The Lively Science: Remodeling Human Social Research* it is. In the next two chapters, I'd like to start out by looking a little more closely at three of the 19th century founders. The first, John Stuart Mill, actually lays the groundwork for BSS, but in a way that aims at HSR as well. The second, Franz Brentano, hangs onto BSS but muddies things up by including the minds of subjects. Then the third, Wilhelm Dilthey, breaks with BSS completely and argues, as does this book, that HSR is a different kind of science.

Any one of these three alone could fill a lifetime of scholarship. Books and articles about all of them litter the academic landscape. And these three are not the only possible choices for an HSR type like me to look at for historical roots. I think if I were starting life over again I'd study them all for years. In my day in graduate school we heard their names mostly as footnotes, if at all.

After dealing with the foundational figures, a second part of the book will ask: Given that the science has to be different, how can we think about evidence, logic and falsification in a way that fits the study of human beings better but is still "scientific?" A third part will then look at a major issue that BSS hides with its delusional notions of "objectivity." Human social science involves human funders, human researchers, human subjects and human audiences communicating with each other across the boundaries of their different worlds. How do we come to terms with these multiple and intersecting worlds as evidence is gathered and logic applied? Finally, at the end of the book, the broader context of human social science will be explored with the classic BSS research of Milgram, as already promised, showing the HSR threads that weave through it, along with some final consideration of the many interests at play in the field of human social research.

The next chapter is the most difficult in the book. It's probably a poor choice of writing strategy to start that way. But John Stuart

Mill lays the groundwork for mainstream human social science and at the same time foreshadows the problems that HSR will address. His work represents the foundations, the problems, and an introduction to the way solutions will start to take shape. If it gets to be too much skip ahead to Chapter Three and read on for awhile and then go back.

As they say in Spanish slang when it's time to get going, dále gas, which means "give it gas." My colleague from University of Houston days, Max Martinez, San Antonio pandillero turned professor of creative writing, used to say that all the time when he wanted departmental debates to get to the point. Given the nature of those debates, Max said it a lot.

Just for fun, right after I wrote those lines, thinking of Max, I looked on the Internet. There is a song called "Dále Gas," done by several groups. This one is from a version by the Dikers. Here is how it starts:

> Olvidar todo lo que queda atrás, si estuvo bien o fue fatal, nunca me resulta fácil. Esperar siempre se me dió muy mal, mientras los fantasmas ríen a mi espalda.

In my bad idiomatic translation:

> Forgetting the past, whether it was good or awful, it's never easy for me. Just waiting and hoping all the time bums me out, while ghosts laugh behind my back.

Then comes the refrain, dále gas, dále gas … That's more or less the attitude behind this book.

CHAPTER TWO

Experiments and Real Worlds

John Stuart Mill (1806-1873) was no academic wallflower. This giant of Western intellectual history was a liberal political philosopher and a utilitarian, advocating the greatest good for the greatest number of people. He worked as a colonial administrator in India and served as a Member of Parliament in addition to his academic positions. He continually engaged in social reform and argued for an early version of feminism.

When he wrote about some things, like political economy, he argued very much in the spirit of HSR. For example, he pointed out to the economists of the time that people usually have motives in addition to personal economic gain when they buy and sell. And, in his reformist mode, he showed how institutions were as important in understanding economic behaviors as were individual acts. Those institutions could be changed through political action. He might be speaking to us now as financial regulatory reform born of the 2008 recession animates the talking heads in our news media. If he applied for a research grant today, reviewers at NSF and NIH would probably say that his politics are too explicit and that he's much too applied.

So I'm a little upset to tell you, for all the good advice he gave and as much as I admire him for so many things, he was one of the main architects of the BSS high-rise that isolated its occupants from the world they were supposed to be figuring out. But I'm also happy to tell you that the logic he invented, if we liven it up a little, serves as a building block for HSR as well.

Mill described a fundamental human ability that drives science to this day—the famous *induction*. He called it "the discovery of all truths not self-evident" (pg. 231—page references in this chapter refer to his book cited in the chapter notes). He then invented different versions of a logic to turn this ability into a science, *inductive logic*. The BSS error was to take this useful idea and claim there was only one version of it worth using and only one way to use it, like inventing Velcro and saying it only works on shoes. Let's start with the basics of Mill's logic.

One thing that humans are good at, an ability that science in fact builds on, is induction. Induction means, in its simplest form, that humans notice that when one thing occurs, so does another thing, and then they *generalize* the observation. Not just humans can do this. Animals do it all the time, too, as any pet-owner or rancher knows. Like Pavlov's dogs—bell and food, bell and food, pretty soon ring the bell and the dog salivates.

But Mill was right to worry about the seduction of induction. People may be good at spotting co-occurrences of X and Y, but they're also good at *only* seeing cases that support the generalization they make as a result. And they're not bad at explaining away cases that seem to contradict it, either. With a little selective perception and creative interpretation, it turns out a contradictory case can easily be made to look like a supportive one.

Mill worried because the way humans notice X and Y, both the first time and then later, is subject to all kinds of social pressures and psychological errors. For example, most readers will have seen articles on the ever-growing list of "biases" that steer our everyday judgments. Look at "List of Cognitive Biases" on Wikipedia to get started if you're curious. Daniel Kahnemann, one of the pioneers, recently published a readable book, *Thinking Fast and Slow*, which lays out the story of the field.

I'll use one venerable example here, the well-known *cognitive dissonance*. Leon Festinger coined that term in his 1956 book, *When Prophecy Fails*. It's dated, but then again, Paul Krugman just used the book title and the concept for his *New York Times* column on December 24, 2012. How, Festinger wondered, would a group who predicted the end of the world handle it when the world didn't end? They handled it just fine, as it turned out, working things around as to how their very concern so impressed the powers-that-be that those powers decided to give the group, and the world, another chance. The fact that the world stayed put didn't prove them wrong after all. It actually proved them right.

My favorite example of this kind of thing is the apocryphal story about the flat-earther who said, when shown a picture from an Apollo space flight, "You know, it's amazing how to the untrained eye the earth appears to be round."

The ability to eliminate cognitive dissonance by changing perception of what happens in the world names one of many reasons why a simple induction from a couple of experiences does not a science make. If everything that happens confirms your original induction, then you might as well run for Pope.

Since the rise of the human fallibility industry in psychology, the long list of biases that have been named gets downright depressing if your self-esteem depends on rationality. For example, the "confirmation bias," a modern descendant of cognitive dissonance theory, names the tendency to see only things that support what you already believe. "Loss aversion," another famous example, names our tendency to fear loss more than we value gain. The list goes on and on, now institutionalized in new fields like behavioral economics. We're not as rational as the dismal economists thought we were. There are even mutual funds based on our foibles now.

If you induce and then make everything that happens support what you already believe, there won't be much science going on. Science means the opposite. You do everything you can to show how what you think is going on might be *wrong*. Mill didn't mince words about those who ignored that part of the induction job. He writes that the tendency to ignore contrary cases "is natural to the mind when unaccustomed to scientific methods." It causes people to "accept the facts which present themselves without taking the trouble of searching for more." And he said, "[W]e must have reason to believe that if there were in nature any instances to the contrary, we should have known of them" (pg. 253). We need, in other words, some kind of a *logic*—a guideline for thinking—to convert our natural ability to induce into a science. Mill set out to create one that would do the job.

Notice, by the way, that Festinger and his co-authors did *not* do controlled experiments or standardized social surveys to discover cognitive dissonance. He and his colleagues went out into the world of a small group they were interested in. They saw what happened when the world didn't end, in living color, up close and personal. They created a brand new concept based on first-hand experience with people in the course of their real social life. This study, one of the most important in the history of human social science, got away with being an HSR project in a BSS world.

The Logic

In order to turn a powerful human ability—induction—into a science, John Stuart Mill designed an inductive logic. Not only did he require a scientist—or any critical thinker for that matter—to *notice* cases that didn't fit. He wanted them to do everything in their power to *make problem cases happen*. A full exposition of the book where he blazed the trail, the two-volume *A System of Logic, Ratiocinative and Inductive,* would be impossible here. In fact, a full summary just of the part called "Of Induction," would be as well. But I'll try to summarize the heart of the logic by drawing on that single substantial section.

Mill describes several kinds of induction. Two of the stars in his logic firmament are named the "Method of Agreement" and the "Method of Difference." The Method of Difference is the pinnacle, the top of the line. It is the path to the BSS gold standard, the clinical trial, the experimental design. It is the *real* science. The Method of Agreement, on the other hand, leads to a version that we can sand and polish and use in HSR, and we'll get to it in a moment. First, though, let's deal with the BSS dream.

To use Mill's Method of Difference you need several cases to compare with each other. *The cases have to be identical with each other in every way but one.* The only difference among them is whether or not some factor X is present. In some cases it is; in others, it isn't. If those situations where X is present *always* show some factor Y as well, and if those situations where X is absent *never* show Y, then you're onto a *causal* relationship between X and Y.

You see how the Method of Difference shaped the BSS dream? A scientist needs a series of situations that are exactly the same in all possible ways except for the one thing, the presence or absence of X. There will be an *experimental* group where X is present and a *control* group where it is absent. Obviously, wrote Mill, the scientist is going to have to design those situations and control them, because the real world is too messy, with way too many things going on in any given case.

But if you can build that hermetically sealed world, then once the results are in, no escape is possible. If it didn't work, it didn't work. The only way to weasel out of negative results is to come up with something else that you missed the first time around, some other X that varied that you didn't know was there. But with the perfect Method of Difference, that shouldn't have happened, because there weren't any other X's that could have varied.

Mill knew how demanding the Method of Difference was. At one point he wrote:

> In the spontaneous operations of nature there is generally such complication and such obscurity, they are mostly either so overwhelmingly large or on so inaccessibly minute a scale, we are so ignorant of a great part of the facts which really take place, and even those of which we are not ignorant are so multitudinous, and therefore so seldom exactly alike in any two cases, that a spontaneous experiment of the kind required by the Method of Difference, is commonly not to be found (pg. 311).

In other words, forget the real world. The controlled lab is the only hope here. He writes mostly with an eye on natural science. Now and then he mentions human social science, and when he does, even lab experiments look pretty hopeless. With a human situation at any given moment "…it will be surrounded and obscured by an indefinite multitude of unascertainable circumstances, rendering the use of the common experimental methods almost delusive" (pg. 303). He mentions that the same is true for studies of society and the state as well as of the individual.

This is an important historical moment in terms of where *The Lively Science* is going. In spite of the problems he described, Mill's Method of Difference remains, still today, the gold standard for mainstream BSS. It is institutionalized. Consider two of the primary funding sources in the U.S.: The National Institutes of Health, as the medical name suggests, celebrates "clinical trials" as its mark of prestige. The National Science Foundation, dominated as it is by natural science, does the same with the "experimental method," essentially the same thing. But didn't Mill say the gold standard was a pipe dream for individuals, societies and states? It's hard to read him any other way.

Are you feeling the double bind here, the "catch-22" if you're old enough to remember Joseph Heller's novel? The perfect human social science means you have to do something that is impossible to do, said by a father figure of scientific research? Gregory Bateson created a theory of schizophrenia based on exactly this kind of family experience.

As noted previously, Mill developed other versions of inductive logic. None of them had the horsepower of the gold standard, he said, but a different version— the Method of Agreement— worked pretty well without the lab. Maybe you couldn't control the world, but you could organize the material it provided when you paid attention to it. Now I'd like to take a look at that version of his logic, because it's a logic that HSR can use. I'll introduce it here and then in Chapter Five I'll bring it up to date and put an engine in it so that we can drive it through time and across a lot of different kinds of data, including data about the researcher and the research itself.

Out of the Lab

If observation of those erratic humans as they take care of business is all you have, what next? Are you just up the scientific creek without a logical paddle?

Of course not. Enter the Method of Agreement, a more congenial sounding alternative. It works fine with "observations." The Method of Agreement is simple. If two or more instances of some phenomenon Y have some X in common, and you keep seeing this over and over again, then X and Y have some kind of connection, though it's not at all clear what that connection is or what other things might make X or Y happen separately from each other. At least we can learn *something* from observation. This kind of induction should sound familiar, if a reader recalls how the chapter began. It is the kind that humans naturally do, and, as we've seen, it has serious problems as a science.

So Mill fixed that problem, to some extent, by combining "difference" and "agreement" into a single version of inductive logic. He added a requirement to the original Method of Agreement and said you had to go forth in the world and find cases that didn't work as well. In fact, a century or so after Mill, contemporary HSR and BSS types would both talk about the possibility of "natural experiments," that is, ways to find and organize variation out in the world that is already there. The logic for these natural experiments was so close to the unrealistic Method of Difference that Mill sometimes called it the "*Indirect* Method of Difference." Unfortunately, he didn't call it that much, so it comes down to us under the awkward name he preferred, the "Joint Method of Agreement and Difference." I'll just call it the "joint method" here, no allusion to controlled substances intended. This one is so important to *The Lively Science* that I'll quote it in Mill's own words, from page 315 of his *Logic*.

> If two or more instances in which the phenomenon occurs have only one circumstance in common, while two or more instances in which it does not occur have nothing in common save the absence of that circumstance, the circumstance in which alone the two sets of instances differ, is the effect, or the cause, or an indispensable part of the cause, of the phenomenon.

Mill's joint method corrects the original problem of just noticing "agreement," that human tendency to stick with the positive cases where X and Y occur together and then call it an inductive day and wave away the counterexamples. He foregrounds the scientific responsibility to look for the *negative* cases, the ones that do *not* fit the induction, the ones that the desire to resolve cognitive dissonance and other mental tricks and social pressures stand ready to explain away.

Here is a picture of how the joint method works. Take a simple two by two table, like the example below, with X and Y being either present or absent. The natural human induction is to notice the "X and Y present" cell, the upper left in the diagram. It's not a bad ability to have if you're trying to make it through the day. If X and Y are really joined at the hip, though, then the two cells that show "one is present/the other is absent"—the lower left and upper right—should be empty. More than that, as the lower right hand cell of the table shows, if you don't get one, then you can *never* get the other. If X and Y are *always* present and *always* absent together, then you have closed in on the traditional gold standard dream, even without an experiment.

	Y Present	Y Absent
X Present	Many	None
X Absent	None	Many

The other day I stopped to talk with an acquaintance at the community college. He was looking at a CNN feature on a TV screen hanging from the ceiling. The feature warned against the dangers of skin cancer from exposure to the sun. He turned to me and said that he had three relatives who never went in the sun and they all died of skin cancer. This whole CNN feature was just bullshit, he said.

Look at the diagram of Mill's logic again. My acquaintance heard the TV as saying *all* cases are in the X present and Y present box. His relatives were in the X absent Y present box. Therefore cases in the X present and Y present box were—I don't know what he thought, maybe scare tactics supported by the sunscreen lobby. I drew him a version of the above diagram. He seemed happy enough that he had discovered a box that CNN was concealing from the public. He wasn't bothered at all that he and CNN both were examples of how quickly humans induce, how unscientifically they do it, and how they could care less about the other boxes in Mill's logic and the way they might complicate things.

In the end, Mill's Method of Difference, the version of his logic that requires laboratory control, became the heart and soul of BSS, the tabernacle where the gold standard of clinical trials and the experimental method were kept. Mill himself, had he been a consultant to NIH and NSF, might have advised them to think this through a little more carefully first. The good news for *The Lively Science*, though, is that the Method of Difference is not the only game in town. We're going to run with that second version of Mill's work on induction, *the joint method.* The joint method works for "observation" as well as experiment, observation being a code word here for actually engaging the phenomenon that a human social science has to describe and explain, namely human subjects like us leading our lives in social worlds not entirely of our own making.

Buying a Car

Mill's definition of the joint method only takes a few cases to get started—"two or more" for each condition he says. All that is to the good. The logic doesn't say you have to define the sample *before* you start, like BSS does. You can build it as you go, an HSR specialty, by the way. In fact, Mill offered good HSR advice when he said that the greater the variety among the cases that you apply the logic to, the better. And, he added, you really shouldn't get too carried away with large numbers. Instead, you should pick cases that you've learned might be critical in proving yourself wrong based on what you know at the point when you make the choice. Mill's logic, to twist the old saying, is an HSR dog that can hunt. He is much more flexible than the modern versions of BSS sampling would lead you to believe.

Look back at Mill's definition of the joint method again. Look at the details of what those cases have to be like when you put X and Y to the test. The *only* thing that the positive cases can have in common is that X and Y are *both present,* preferably in a clear and rapid sequence where X happens and then Y happens. And the *only* thing that the negative cases can have in common is that X and Y are *both absent.* One never happens when the other doesn't. In the actual human social world, cases as simple as these are as rare as an honest politician.

The problem is, in the real human social world, there are

always a lot more things going on than just an X and a Y, and those other things interact with both of them as well. Nothing new here. Mill said the same thing. So now we've got a choice to make. Do we, the researchers, create some situation where we think that only X and Y can possibly be relevant? That is the BSS experimental dream based on the Method of Difference. Or do we give up on the laboratory and take a look at the much more complicated—and realistic—situation we are interested in out there in the human social world? That's the HSR goal.

How can we strive for that goal and still say we're doing science? In this section, let's look at an example to show what a wicked thing this simple problem is. Say we want to explain a simple choice, like a decision to buy a particular car. Say I'm one of the cases, one of the "data points." The researcher has to get data from me. Say the Y means buying a particular car. What is the X that causes me to do that?

When I moved to New Mexico, I bought a Subaru Forester. Embarrassing—an amazing number of Subarus ply New Mexico roads—but there it is. That's the Y, what BSS calls the "dependent variable." Now, what "independent variable" should I look at, the X that always happens with Y but never happens when Y isn't there? Subaru's marketing department wants to know and they're willing to pay an exorbitant amount of money if a researcher can answer their question.

Here's an induction that an airport employee actually made. A while ago I flew home to Albuquerque and the parking shuttle driver offered a peculiar hypothesis. I didn't ask him; he just came out with it after I pointed out my car. "Yeah," he said, "people who travel a lot drive either Subarus or hybrids." Why he thought I travelled a lot was a mystery. Maybe it was the thousand-yard stare that comes from sitting in airborne sardine cans.

If he'd read John Stuart Mill, though, he'd wonder right away if people who do *not* travel a lot also do *not* drive Subarus. (I'll leave the hybrids out of it for now). And he'd wonder about the people who travel a lot and drive something else, and the people who drive Subarus—what one mystery writer called "the national car of Santa Fe"—who don't travel much at all. So far so good— the joint method applied in a straightforward way to complicate an induction. Mill's logic guides us to many cases that will falsify the shuttle driver's hypothesis. In fact, it will pretty much shred it and leave us with no clear X/Y induction at all.

Frequent travel out of the Albuquerque airport is not why I bought a Forester. I bought it because it had a good quality record, because it had room to haul junk around since I became a first-time homeowner when I moved to New Mexico, because it had all-wheel drive for snow and mud in the country, because my mother left me some money so I could afford paying more than I ever had before for a car, because it had a moon roof and a compass, and because I didn't want to waste more time looking for a car, all of which finally overrode the embarrassment of buying a bourgeois suburban conservative ride instead of the Corvette that was the dream car of my youth that I couldn't afford anyway. A lot of X's and Y's going on, and a lot of others *not* going on, and I'm just getting started.

Mill's logic would have kept the shuttle driver from a wrong-headed induction, but it's not getting us to a science, either. In fact, it's suggesting that maybe I'm suffering delusions of grandeur if I think I could ever make a science out of this mess. I'm nowhere near a conclusion that will get me Subaru's corporate money, but I'm learning something about buying their car, aren't I?

Ecological Validity

Mill and I aren't the only ones to question whether science is possible here. John Gaddis wrote a book called The *Landscape of History* to explain how historians worked. He said he had always had trouble understanding why he didn't get along well with his BSS colleagues. Then one day, while writing the book, it hit him. They kept asking him what his "independent" variable was. In the human social world, he said, there aren't any. There are just herds of interacting variables influencing each other as they move along through time and now and then produce surprises. Eric Hobsbawm, another historian, wrote a book late in life where he wondered how come no one had known the variables to predict the most powerful events of the 20th century before they happened? And, as John Stuart Mill himself put it in his Victorian way, which I paraphrase, out there in the world a lot of causes are in play and a lot of different effects could have been produced by any one of them.

Mill was discouraged about the possibility of a human social science. John Mackie, in his encyclopedia article about Mill, wrote that he considered it "gappy." Mackie meant that there are just too many variables to ever get scientific control over them all. And, true enough, there will always be "gaps" stuffed with uncontrolled variables. Mill concluded that human social science was still worth doing, though, kind of like weather forecasting, an amazing premonition on his part that foreshadows complexity and chaos theory, about which more in a moment. Weather, as we all complain in our small talk because no one will ever disagree, surprises us all the time. All sorts of variables mess with each other in complicated ways, so who could expect it to be otherwise? But we still try to forecast the weather, and we are getting better and better at it, at least in the short term.

No wonder President Truman and the poet Auden and the writer Mark Twain had problems with human social science, if a reader remembers how this book opened in Chapter One. John Stuart Mill already saw it coming. There are too many variables interacting in too many ways out there in the real world. Contemporary BSS types recognize the problem as well. They sum up this "gappiness" as a problem of *ecological validity*, a snappy way of asking, "what does this correlation in my data have to do with all those variables that got left behind on the way to the lab?"

The most frequently cited source for this BSS epiphany is Ulric Neisser's book *Cognition and Reality*. But the clearest definition I found was in a web-based glossary. I'll italicize key lines in the quote below. And notice that this isn't some anti-science tirade at the Poststructural Bar and Grill. This is psychology talking to itself about what it does:

> Ecological Validity: Ecological Validity is the degree to which the behaviors observed and recorded in a study reflect the behaviors that actually occur in natural settings. In addition, ecological validity is associated with "generalizability". Essentially this is the extent to which findings (from a study) can be generalized (or extended) to the "real world." *In virtually all studies there is a trade-off between experimental control and ecological validity. The more control psychologists exert in a study, typically the less ecological validity and thus, the less they may be able to generalize.* For example, when we take people out of their natural environment and study them in the lab, we are exerting some control over them and, as a result, possibly limiting how much we can generalize the findings to all people in natural settings.

It's an even more serious question than that, though. It's not just "What do the results of our experiment or survey have to do with what goes on out there in the real world?" It's "Why didn't we just look at the real world in the first place?"

The BSS answer is, we *have* to work the way that we do; we couldn't claim to do science otherwise. The real world is too complicated, too messy, too loosely wrapped. Echoes of John Stuart Mill. The HSR response: It's not that you *can't* do science. It's that you're trying to do the science the *wrong way*. The real human social world isn't a lab. But it isn't random, either. The late Dell Hymes, grand old man of linguistic anthropology, used to joke with those who thought researching real life was too complicated a goal to aspire to. After a paper on the impossibility of figuring out the human social world was offered at a conference we both attended, Hymes said to the presenter, "You got here, didn't you?"

My convoluted path to a Subaru Forster purchase didn't fit into a simple inductive logic diagram. But there was something in there that Subaru might use about their customers. It wasn't useless information. The question for HSR is, how do we handle that "gappy" part of the world and still have a science?

The first time I went to London and rode the Tube, the recorded public service announcement warned riders about the space between the train and the platform. "Mind the gap," it said. Words to live by, I thought at the time.

The Heartbreak of Timeless Reduction

What do we do about this problem of ecological validity? How do we turn the real world into a scientific object and not lose its reality in the process? The question is at the heart of *The Lively Science*.

As usual, Mill was ahead of his time, as I already mentioned, when he speculated that "social science" might be more like "weather forecasting" than like traditional science. He was ahead of his time because the issues he raised about multiple causes and multiple effects would become central in the sciences of chaos and complexity that blossomed in the latter part of the 20th century. Weather forecasting was in fact a prime source of the new ideas that inspired it.

In 1963 a meteorologist named Edward Lorenz published an article in an obscure professional journal. The damnedest thing had happened. He was running weather simulations on one of the room-sized computers of the day. If you kept the input variables the same, you could run the thing a million times and get the same results. But then one day he stopped a run in the middle and went off to do whatever weather-people do when they take a break, probably look out the window and wonder why in the hell it had all of a sudden started raining. Then he put his coffee cup back in the sink and returned to the computer and rounded off the numbers in the simulation where he had stopped it. We're talking about a *very* small difference between the numbers when it stopped and the numbers when he re-started the computer. He typed in the new numbers and the simulation picked up where it had left off. Except that, even with that tiny difference, the simulation all of a sudden spun off into a very different kind of weather.

This just didn't make any sense. A small change in the numbers maybe could produce a small change in what the simulation did from that point forward. But this—it was almost like the computer had a mind of its own. A few years later, in 1969, he published another article that coined the phrase, now a cliché, the "*butterfly effect*," the idea that an unexpected trivial event, like a small difference in a number, could have major effects on what a system as a whole did as it continued its march through time. A butterfly flaps its wings in the tropics and causes a hurricane in the Gulf of Mexico. Every time I hear the cliché I think of the old rock group, *Iron Butterfly*.

Lorenz, recently deceased, is now honored as a patron saint of what is called "nonlinear dynamic systems," popularly known as "chaos" and "complexity." Mill, of course, couldn't have known about it during his day, though he was aware of the 19th century French mathematician Poincaré, who was already working on the "three body problem," the Franco-Newtonian version of a physics *ménage a trois*. The three-body problem was this: Newton's equations worked fine with *two* planets. Add a third and the *interactions* among the three made it impossible to calculate the results. Poincaré came up with an early version of chaos theory, and I now have a plastic statue of him on the dashboard of my Subaru.

Three bodies and surprising weather are the natural science versions of the "gappy" problem that Mill foresaw for human social science. But it is worse than Mill thought. It is way past just being "gappy." It's not only about the *number* of variables. The problem is that the human social world, like the natural world that produces our weather, is loaded with many *interacting* variables. They interact in countless ways, including feedback loops where a little change can blow up into a big change—what Lorenz discovered with his weather simulation—or a big change can get squashed into nothing—like when you try and alter procedures in a university bureaucracy.

HSR research is like studying the weather, in the sense that the human social world is also a nonlinear dynamic system. That world is loaded with interacting variables. This fact has to be part of its epistemology, or else it cannot be a science at all. It's a major reason for the ecological validity problem of most BSS. The human social world is nonlinear and dynamic. The lab experiment is not.

More on chaos and complexity as the book goes on.

Reductionism

Before we go nonlinear, though, I want to describe Mill's own 19th century solution for "gappy" social science, a solution that, sad to say, shows how far off he was. It was as linear and non-dynamic as it could be. In fact, this is where Mill heads north where HSR needs to turn south. His solution is called *reductionism*. It claims that science can explain a system as a simple sum of its parts. Reality is complicated, but we scientists can untangle it into its pieces, nail it down one piece at a time, and add them up. True, there are many causes and many effects, but Mill wrote:

> ...the regularity which exists in nature is a web composed of distinct threads, and only to be understood by tracing each of the threads separately; for which purpose it is often necessary to unravel some portion of the web, and exhibit the fibers apart. The rules of experimental inquiry are the contrivances for unraveling the web (pg. 259).

Say you're landing an airplane. Speed and direction are caused by the engine and the steering. But there's also a crosswind with a different speed and direction. No worries, you reduce the problem to its two elements, plane and crosswind. The plane steers in a way that adapts to the sum of the two causes, and a pilot can adjust to land on the runway instead of Row D of long-term parking. Reductionism pure and simple. Sum up the two causes and you get the observed effect.

For a simple human example, return to the Subaru purchase. Reductionism might say, there are ten things about a car that a customer looks at. Add up how the customer feels about each of those ten things and you get a score that tells you how likely he is to buy the car. It might work to some extent. Until you pass addition and move into multiplication—a moon roof and a compass are worth way more together than they are separately. Or into what isn't on the list but changes all its values, like a pushy salesman means the customer is out of there. Or into feedback loops, like if the buyer has to look at one more car in this oversaturated consumer jungle he's going to move to Amsterdam and buy a bicycle.

Mill knows there are problems here and he discusses them at length, though in the end he stays with reduction as the bedrock of science. Let me summarize some of the criticisms he considered as a preview of what is to come in the rest of this book. What he—and his BSS progeny—want to get rid of, i.e., the interacting and complicating variables in human social worlds, HSR wants to include and figure out as part of the science.

One of Mill's critics, William Whewell, another fascinating 19th century figure, argues that some things just can't be broken down into parts and still be that thing. As Mill writes:

> Dr. Whewell maintains that the general proposition which binds together the particular facts and makes them, as it were, one fact, is not the mere sum of those facts, but something more, since there is introduced a conception of the mind which did not exist in the facts themselves (pg. 240).

As my precocious rural grandniece might put it, "My chicken is more than a collection of feathers."

This is the old "whole is more than the sum of its parts" argument. To rephrase it in the way that annoys Mill, the whole cannot be *reduced* to its parts. Sure, the whole is made up of parts.

And the whole for sure has a part or two that, if you break it, the whole won't work. Think of the Subaru again. But the car isn't just a *sum* of those car parts. The Subaru whole that is made up of car parts is different from other cars that are made up of essentially the same things.

This same glitch comes up again when Mill discusses chemistry. Chemical combinations, he notes, can produce something "with properties entirely different from those of either of the two substances separately" (pg. 291), as in the example of hydrogen and oxygen combining to produce water, or sodium and chloride producing salt. Though he recognizes that this kind of thing represents "one of the fundamental distinctions in nature," he argues around it to conclude that his reductionist version of cause and effect still works most of the time. But clearly, chemical combinations represent a result that is more than the sum of their parts, and he knows it.

This "part/whole" business opens a door into a room with no floor. There is a long philosophical tradition, called "mereology," from the Greek for "study of parts." Head for the entry in the on-line *Stanford Encyclopedia of Philosophy* if you want to get started. And, in fact, some of mereology's modern development comes from the 19th century founders of HSR who will appear in the next chapter. We don't need mereology for purposes of this book, but we do need some way to talk about these wholes. I'll use the straightforward word *pattern* here, in the sense that a pattern is of course made up of parts, but it is more than just a list of them.

Remember the Subaru purchase? Reductionism didn't work. A variable—a single car attribute—didn't cause another variable—a purchase by me. I bought a car that fit pretty well into my life, also partly because I was just worn out shopping for cars. Just for fun, to celebrate New Year's Day 2013 as I revised this book for the last time, after I'd already written all the bits about Subaru in this chapter, I looked on the web to see what Subaru's marketing people might really have said about why people buy their car. In an article in U.S. News and World Report in 2009, Katy Marquardt reports that

> ... the company's marketing director describes Subaru owners as "the types who collect experiences rather than things; they tend to be very environmentally aware and socially involved."

And in a later quote:

> But the brand, perhaps better known as the wagon of choice for the progressive set, is also in the unusual position of being a non-luxury brand that appeals to those who can afford a Mercedes or BMW.

That was really annoying to read. How dare they call me an experience-collecting, environmentally aware, socially involved progressive who could have bought a Beemer. As the old joke goes, I resemble that remark. Except for the Beemer. I'd rather have a Corvette.

After I found this quote, I understood why it is that, in the last couple of decades, HSR took off in fields like marketing research and consumer product design, and why companies like Xerox and Intel pioneered the use of HSR groups to look at people using their technology in their everyday lives, or not using it where they might be able to.

Subaru's marketing department wasn't trying to find a variable that causes a person to want a particular car. They were finding patterns of everyday life where their particular model of car fit in as a part of that pattern, and then making that case to potential customers who lived that way. As I write this, I realize why it is I find the TV show *Mad Men* so fascinating.

BSS gets its turn in this game, though, and foreshadows how the two—HSR and BSS—can have useful disagreements. "Fine, Subaru," says BSS, "you sell the car by fitting it to a pattern. Are you saying that the pattern *causes* the sale? If you are, then return to Mill's inductive logic boxes and tell me about people without the pattern who buy the car and people with the pattern that buy a different car and you can learn something from those other boxes to expand your market."

Then Subaru says, "Never mind your little boxes. Our company had one of the few automobiles whose sales actually increased during the recession. The 'pattern present/sold the Subaru' box is good enough for us."

Then I can picture *Mad Men* star Don Draper saying, "I want the whole market" and he leaves the room and goes back to his office and pours a scotch and waits for their call.

There are scenes in the series episodes that kind of look like this.

Mill wants to rule out this notion of pattern as more than its parts. The problem with his argument is that figuring out patterns is much of what HSR does. It's the pattern, not its pieces, that is the goal of the science. It is about creating a concept from a researcher's point of view that pulls together the pieces of what is going on in a human social world that she is trying to describe and explain.

Remember *When Prophecy Fails*, described earlier in this chapter? What was that cult doing to handle the failure of the world to end like it was supposed to, wondered Leon Festinger.

His answer was a pattern that he named *cognitive dissonance* and then he went on to describe the different ways to resolve it. This HSR project, in turn, bred legions of BSS research, demonstrating the kind of cross-over that we will see in Stanley Milgram's obedience research in the final chapter of this book. The point for now, though, is that for Mill HSR pattern discovery doesn't count as science. For HSR, it is the heart of it. It has everything to do with figuring out what X and Y, and several other interacting things, have to do with each other. Finding patterns is a way to fill in those "gaps" in "gappy" human social science and remain true to the "real" world.

The use of the term "variable" for part of a pattern, and the notion that "cause" is in play as part of it as well— that language can work into any human social science. But those notions are secondary to the discovery of the pattern in the first place. Without the pattern, you don't know which parts interact, and without the interaction, you don't know what matters in the pattern.

Reductionism is a linchpin of Mill's science. It argues that, in the end, all science can be "reduced" to the level of physics. As the famous physicist Ernest Rutherford said in the early 20th century, physics is the only real science. The rest is just stamp collecting. It just goes to show that even Nobel Prize winners say dumb things. I'm pretty sure I didn't buy the Subaru because of gravity or electromagnetic attraction.

The Subaru marketing department is closer to the truth. I bought their car because, after shopping to the point where I couldn't stand it any more, a Subaru suited the pattern of how I lived. You couldn't have predicted my choice from a list of car attributes, because most of those attributes were parts of many other cars. But you could have limited the range of choices I *might* make if you'd learned my pattern first.

To get the range absolutely right, though, the marketing department would have had to know more about my patterns than I've mentioned so far. I grew up in the California Valley and had just moved to a rural community in the Southwestern desert. So I also looked at several four-wheel drive pickup trucks as well. In my case, marketing had more HSR work to do. I'm not the only country and western progressive in the Southwest. So why doesn't Subaru make a pickup? They keep trying. But their current version, the "Sambar?" I'd be the laughing stock of the desert. Maybe the Don Draper character from *Mad Men* could help them out here.

Pattern on Drugs

A science of a few variables frozen in time, where one causes another in a straightforward way, and where causes add up to predict the pattern that includes them—that kind of reductionist approach won't solve John Stuart Mill's "gappy" problem for human social science, it won't produce ecological validity, and it won't get us anywhere near HSR.

In my final drug research project—I left the field in the mid 2000s exhausted by its self-defeating politics—I wanted to explain why illegal drug epidemics kept happening. After years of human social science work of all types, the professionals still didn't know the answer. Reductionist "causes" had been offered of every imaginable sort, causes based on personal characteristics, sometimes biological, and other causes based on society, politics, economics and religion. None of the research predicted worth a damn. Epidemics always surprised everyone with how quickly they appeared, out of nowhere it seemed. BSS, not to mention biology, had failed to either describe or explain them. So had HSR.

In the late 1990s, after decades in the drug field, I walked into the streets of Baltimore and got depressed and angry at this failure. The crack cocaine epidemic was then going on all over the city. Everyone had seen crack coming in the 1980s, sliding down the northeastern corridor from New York, and many dedicated and experienced policy and prevention types had worked very hard to block it. It didn't matter. Crack rolled in and, in the hands of a new distribution system, took off and destroyed lives and neighborhoods. Epidemics like crack seemed to explode on their own and then spread like wildfire.

The reductionist goal of predicting epidemics using causal variables had not worked. Thirty years of the war on drugs and no improvement. I'd just learned a little complexity theory as my project started. Maybe an illegal drug epidemic was a nonlinear dynamic system, a movie with an evolving plot structure that could go in surprising directions, like Lorenz's weather did. Maybe there weren't any simple causes, but different things could happen that locked into a positive feedback loop that moved through time and, among other things, created a pattern of widespread drug dependence.

I wrote a grant to NIH. They kind of liked it but it looked weird. It took two and a half years, but there was a little extra money one year and it was cheap and probably lightening from a thunderstorm caused a computer error, so they funded it.

The results of the seven-year project were not a sound bite, but I can offer a summary. We—me and Heather Reisinger and James Peterson and other colleagues—looked at a lot of different material that no one had put together into the same project before. Not just at the people who became dependent on a substance, but also at what was going on in their world, in various drug markets and production systems, and within the larger world in general.

A fascinating *pattern* emerged—that word again—that was more than just the sum of its parts, that magic result that so annoyed John Stuart Mill when Dr. Whewell described it.

A summary goes like this. On the one hand, an organizational crisis happened somewhere in the world, typically among a criminal or political group. It might be a political movement in need of cash, like the Contras in Central America or the Mujahedeen under Soviet occupation in Afghanistan. Or it might be a drug production system in crisis, like Colombia's cocaine producers when they ran out of affluent customers for powder and figured out a new way to market it for poorer consumers, the inspiration for the invention of crack.

Then some part of the population in the U.S. had to fall into what we called "open marginality," which meant that history had thrown them an unexpected curve. A recent promise wasn't delivered on, or a good situation rapidly deteriorated. The social catastrophe happened rapidly and unexpectedly—a historical hurricane—and it left the population in a situation of psychic and usually economic distress. With crack, two of the most powerful parts of the pattern were: The more affluent residents of inner city neighborhoods left as civil rights legislation opened up U.S. society, and President Reagan's administration pulled federal support out from under U.S. cities. Increasing areas of Baltimore became what one urban planner called "warehouses for the poor."

Then, an optional third event might happen: Global politics and economics might change dramatically so that new migration streams into the U.S. began, streams that represented potential links for distribution from producer to consumer. In the crack case, political violence in Jamaica resulted in an out-migration to the U.S. A few entered the marijuana business, then shifted to crack cocaine and distributed it up and down the Atlantic seaboard.

So here's the illegal drug epidemic movie in outline: A production system, new or in crisis, a population, sucker-punched by history in both a psychological and economic sense, and, possibly, a new migration stream to serve as couriers. If all three of these changes occurred rapidly and at about the same time—around 1980 in the case of crack— and if—a big "if"—the changes linked up so that a positive feedback loop snapped into focus among the three elements, then the conditions for an illegal drug epidemic to develop were in place. The emergence of the loop didn't guarantee that an epidemic would happen though—other contingencies and connections had to come together that I'm not describing here—but those conditions set up the pattern that might, and in the case of crack did, lead to a drug explosion.

In a gift to the project that I would rather not have received, a heroin epidemic surprised us and everyone else in the U.S. even as we started work in the late 1990s. A wave of heroin *use* (not addiction, not at first) hit the Baltimore metropolitan area and it rapidly spread to neighborhoods and suburbs that hadn't seen use before. The story was, the crack cocaine market had flattened out, so cocaine producers in Latin America imported and began to cultivate opium poppies to develop a new product, namely, heroin. They dropped the heroin into their established crack distribution system that ran up and down the East Coast and marketed it aggressively as a "loss leader" to new markets, like suburban youth.

Heroin became trendy among Baltimore youth for a year or so and then lost its novelty. But, the *addicts* that the wave left behind emerged in the white working class section of the city, the section where, for the first time in several generations, the kids were doing worse than their parents. The full story was more complicated than this brief summary, but it demonstrated the nonlinear heroin epidemic movie plot even as we worked to discover it in historical cases—an organizational crisis in a production system, a population dropped by history into open marginality, and a distribution system, in this case already in place. The pieces of the pattern formed into a loop, fed on each other, and heroin became the new drug *du jour* among populations in places it had not been before.

We called our work a "trend theory." I'm proud of the work and felt, when it was done, that I could leave the drug field with one answer to the classic question of public health epidemiology, "Why these people in this place at this time?" The answer worked for several cases, the ones we studied, ones we read about, and others that international colleagues described to us. It worked because we gave up trying to predict an epidemic with individual and social variables and instead figured out what the pattern of a heroin epidemic looked like. The pattern was about interacting changes among several different human social worlds.

But notice that we only looked at *positive* cases, epidemics that did in fact take off. Good enough to come up with a pattern, but not good enough to test it in all those inductive ways that John Stuart Mill insisted on. We were like the Subaru marketers—we looked for the pattern that the product fit. I ran out of energy by the time we figured it out. But we left the trend theory behind as a challenge for anyone who wasn't as burned out as I was. Go forth and falsify, I thought at the time.

You can read about the major cases we worked on in a book called *Dope Double Agent: The Naked Emperor on Drugs,* my farewell to the drug field. For purposes of this book, though, notice how different the trend theory results were from the causal and reductionist approach that BSS inherited from John Stuart Mill. There is no simple causation. There are moments of cause in the story, but no single one explains the epidemic. An epidemic is not *reduced* to the sum of events. Rather, interacting events over time make it possible, but in order for it to emerge, the events have to link up into feedback loops, which they won't necessarily do, and then all sorts of contingencies have to play out in a certain way for the loop to send the epidemic curve skyward. And to get clear on what some of the contingencies are and how they affect each other, one moment in time won't be enough. The pattern is *dynamic.* It develops *over time* if it develops at all.

The nonlinear dynamic concept changes the idea of prediction. With BSS, numbers are assigned to variables and the future is calculated with an equation. Predictions are made, even if they are incorrect most of the time. With HSR, we can't predict a specific event with certainty, which makes sense given all those variables and their interactions. What we can do is show how several events interact to produce a system that emerges and then changes from one time to the next and sometimes produces surprises. Like the weather. Like the stock market. The result? We can *predict a space of possibilities,* and we can show how if you were at one point in that space you could make a good guess about the next nearby point and react accordingly. In the drug case, for example, you could make a good call as to where to put your limited social service dollars in the short term—education, prevention, early intervention, or treatment—based on what kind of shape the epidemic was taking at that moment, and then you could shift the allocation depending on where it went next.

Nonlinear dynamic HSR is a humbler kind of science in terms of human control, but a wiser kind of science in terms of understanding how the world works and how humans can work more effectively as part of it. In the case of trend theory, we figured out a truly innovative way, he said modestly, to keep an eye out for potential epidemics, together with ways to intervene based on what was going on as they developed, if they did—sort of a "hurricane watch" system for illegal drug weather. Local treatment and prevention staff to whom we showed the concept loved it. We looked around for funds to try it on a small scale in Baltimore. The research funders said it was too applied and the applied funders said it was too much of a research project. At that point, after decades in the drug field, I called it a day and moved on.

Weather forecasting anyone?

Cause

Many are the ways that Mill discusses "cause," only some of which have been described in this book. Doesn't cause play some role in all this pattern business? Of course it does. Here's an easy example: A single powerful X can in fact be a major and immediate "cause" for some Y that a researcher wants to explain. With such powerful causes, a researcher doesn't need to get too subtle about interactions and feedback and emergence. It doesn't matter how you "measure" it, because it's so powerful that it will show up no matter where you look. It gets pretty straightforward here. Often it gets down to the basic needs in Abraham Maslow's hierarchy, like that you have to have food to eat and avoid being killed to stay alive. In fact, with cases like these, an HSR and a BSS type, not to mention anyone else who takes even a superficial look at what's going on, would agree on what's causing what.

Consider my paternal great-grandfather. He probably wouldn't have left Ireland were it not for the potato famine. A severe famine *causes* certain results, whoever the victims are, wherever in the world they live, whenever it occurs. A famine means the victims drop to the bottom of Maslow's hierarchy of needs and worry about starving. A serious famine will "cause" a lot of people to emigrate and a lot of others to die.

Then again, who knows what else my great-grandfather did or had done to him? Maybe he robbed a bank or got his brother's wife pregnant and needed to get out of the country even though he had a potato stash. And why did he leave with his first cousin? Why did they pick Chicago as their destination? Why did he turn into a Catholic after all those years in the Church of Ireland? Why did he wind up an alcoholic elevator operator while his cousin's family founded a meatpacking company and got rich and spawned the actor John Agar who married Shirley Temple and got a role in John Ford's movie *Fort Apache*? Not that I'm bitter or anything. The point is, none of that was "caused" by a potato famine.

This is a problem that David Hume made famous long before logic was a gleam in Mill's eye. As Hume wrote in one often cited quote:

> When we look about us towards external objects, and consider the operation of causes, we are never able, in a single instance, to discover any power or necessary connexion; any quality, which binds the effect to the cause, and renders the one an infallible consequence of the other. There is required a medium, which may enable the mind to draw such an inference, if indeed it be drawn by reasoning and argument. What that medium is, I must confess, passes my comprehension; and it is incumbent on those to produce it, who assert that it really exists, and is the origin of all our conclusions concerning matter of fact.

BSS lusts after cause. Deep down in its historical heart, it wants an old-fashioned science type *law*. For example, according to

Newton's formula, an increase in the mass of two objects, or a decrease in the distance between them, increases their gravitational attraction. Without a conclusion that X causes Y, says BSS, there is no science. Hume is game to talk about cause, but before he does, he says, you have to explain what you mean by it in a specific case and you have to describe how it actually works. Mill agrees in his discussion of logic, by the way. By Hume's rules, even Newton didn't do so well. How does gravity actually work? Damned if he knew. Einstein didn't come up with curved space until the 20th century.

With a cause like famine, Mill's logic applies in a straightforward way if we want to explain starvation and emigration. We can explain Y in terms of X and then satisfy Hume by explaining *why* one causes the other. Lack of food causes hunger causes need for food and eventual death if that need is not fulfilled. You can stay put and perhaps die or move to where there is food and eat and live. We still can't reach Mill's ironclad induction, though, the one described earlier, the "joint method." People emigrate and die due to causes other than a famine. War, for example. In the language of traditional science, severe famine is *sufficient*, but not *necessary* for those bad things to happen.

The problem for HSR is that most of what a researcher sets out to describe and explain in the human social world won't be linked in a direct way to a single powerful, dramatic and obvious cause. And even when it is, as the story of my ancestor suggests, many other parts of a pattern are in play that turned him from an Irish Protestant potato-farmer into a drunk American Catholic elevator operator, or so goes the family folklore. In fact, a colleague recently published a book that shows how a "disaster"—a single powerful cause—takes very different shapes. Even a massive cause and an obvious effect are part of larger patterns that include them and change how they play out. And odds are, in human social worlds, that pattern will emerge in each case in contingent ways, like the drug epidemics. It will include networks of causation, no question about it, but also patterns and interactions and loops and contingencies. Patterns always include cause, but, in human social science, patterns involve a lot more than that.

Paths Taken, and Not

Complexity and chaos help HSR climb out of the science box that John Stuart Mill built. They help *all* science do this, not just the human social varieties. Don't get me wrong here. Plenty of things do remain comfortably linear and causal in the world. When I turn the key on my Subaru it sends an electric current from the battery to the starter motor. If it doesn't, there are only a few causes to look at to find out why it doesn't work. But the most interesting systems—pretty much all the ones that a human social scientist will look at—will be nonlinear and dynamic, *not* linear and causal and reducible.

The nonlinear part is about all those interacting variables that bothered John Stuart Mill. Those interacting parts will make up a whole that we see as a pattern that can't be reduced into just a pile of its pieces. The pattern is the pieces plus the nonlinear dynamic organization of them. We saw that organization in Lorenz's computer when it changed its weather prediction in major ways just because of a little change in the numbers. And we saw it in the drug trend research when a few historical surprises linked up into a new epidemic of drug dependence. And we saw it in my great-grandfather's biography when he—who would've guessed it?—turned into a Catholic when he hit Chicago. Probably looked around at his new neighborhood and figured if he didn't start making the sign of the cross he was destined for a very lonely life.

It's not just a lot of interacting variables. It's how they *move through time*, to change the weather, to change drug use, to change my relative's religion. The patterns aren't just nonlinear; they are also *dynamic*, something that Mill didn't develop, something that one of the historical figures in the next chapter, Wilhelm Dilthey, will obsess about to a fault. "Dynamic" means motion, change, development. It means moving, not sitting still. And one way that the complexity types talk about this feature of systems is to talk about their *path*.

The topic of path will come up again in this book, but it is worth introducing before I leave this chapter because it—like the "nonlinear" part of "nonlinear dynamics"—changes the way HSR will take shape. A human social system doesn't sit still. In research, we look at it at a particular point in time. But it has a past that we can find out about, where it was different from how it is now. And it keeps on moving even as we research it. And we can check it out again after we're done. We don't just look at it at time T. We look at it at time T – 1 and time T + 1. We learn how those patterns grow and stay and decline and come and go.

HSR doesn't just discover patterns. It discovers how they move and change. The way they move and change over time is the *path* that they take. The thing is—here comes another problem for human social science—there won't be just one possible path. In fact, there will have been several. It might have been sunny instead of raining. The new illegal drug supply might have found no customers because of where it was first marketed. My great-grandfather might have been the one who founded a successful company. Those were also possible paths for the three stories I told.

For a popular depiction of path dependence, rent the movie

Run Lola, Run. It shows the same story three different ways, depending on differences in the initial conditions, sort of Lorenz in living color.

Complexity calls this *path dependence.* The phrase just means that with nonlinear dynamic systems, you always see a path, but it's not identical from one time to the next. Run the system again and you'll see it take a different path. But—and this is an important "but"—the paths will be limited by a bounded *space.* Unless the system blows up or dies off or changes in some revolutionary way, a researcher can describe several paths, and he can use those paths to get an idea of the space that limits them, and then try and figure out what the boundaries of that space are and why they are there.

This may sound like an abstract hallucination, but it will come up again and again in the book. Here's another example, also from my drug research past. When methadone first appeared as a drug to treat heroin addicts back in the 1970s, it was part of President Nixon's "war on drugs" policy. Another part of that policy was to crack down on heroin in foreign sources of production and transshipment, especially Turkey and Marseilles. That action meant that heroin markets in New York dried up. And that change in the market meant that methadone, a synthetic narcotic, became a street drug to fill in the gap. It changed from "medication" in the eyes of the treatment establishment to "dope" in the eyes of the street.

No one expected that. And it wasn't inevitable. It was only one path that the introduction of methadone might have taken, because it is easy to imagine other sets of historical conditions that might have led to other paths. In fact, there is now a concept of "counterfactual history" that works exactly this way. A historian looks at cases, figures out their nonlinear dynamics, and then asks "what if" questions to learn something about other possible path trajectories that were not in the data the historian collected.

An entertaining version of counterfactual history is Robert Harris' novel *Fatherland*, a detective story set in a world guided by the imaginative question, what if Hitler had won?

The path dependence of a nonlinear dynamic system is important to carry forward into HSR epistemology. It radically changes how human social science thinks about *prediction*. Path dependence means that, from where the system is at time T, you can't predict exactly where it will be in the future. It depends on what happens between T and that future. At the same time, by looking at many cases, HSR results will show a *space* that limits possible path trajectories. They will show how you can *expect* a certain range of things to happen. And you can guess that certain things probably never will. Isn't that sort of a prediction? It won't snow in the Sahara. An illegal drug that causes seizures won't take off. My great-grandfather didn't turn into a Hindu.

It is prediction, but in a sense of the term different from BSS. Prediction becomes a description of the limits of the space within which different paths can occur. The limits are set by the rules of scientific research—the way it requires evidence, logic and falsification— and by the human social world within which the research is done—the established meanings, contexts and practices of human subjects as well as the historical conditions that constrain their world. But within those limits, a research strategy and its results can develop along several different possible paths, though not all paths are possible, and it means that the end of the path can look different from one project to another.

BSS implodes in the face of this description. Exact prediction not only vanishes; so does the traditional notion of reliability. The same kind of project could have different results and still be science, because it captures the dynamics of human social worlds and the dynamics of the research that investigates them. From a BSS point of view this is psychotic. Nonlinear dynamics, on the other hand, can handle it just fine. It expects it. Much more discussion of paths to come later in the book, but the concept is worth noticing here as we leave John Stuart Mill for two of the founders of HSR in the next chapter. The concept of prediction, a sacred cow for BSS, mutates into a different kind of science for HSR, an example of the kind of conceptual change that will happen over and over again in this book.

Mill: The Good, the Bad and the Ugly

John Stuart Mill is the required starting point for a discussion of modern human social science, at least in my book, "my book" in both a metaphorical and literal sense. One version of his logic, the Method of Difference, became the gold standard of human social science, the clinical trials and experimental model that BSS has forever celebrated as the impossible dream to which it must aspire.

BSS faced a dilemma when it followed Mill and bought into the Method of Difference as the prestige neighborhood in which to locate their science. By those rules, BSS couldn't be about the actual human social world while at the same time being a science, so it did the only thing it could do. It gave up on the human social world. It pulled people out of that world and put them into controlled and simplified situations of a researcher's design, situations modeled as much as possible on a traditional science lab where the Method of Difference could be imagined to work. It chased the natural science version of reliability but lost ecological validity.

The limits of BSS with respect to what its research represents have been massive and long lasting and it's time for its monopoly to end. A science of humans doing everyday things in their everyday world needs to take data from and test conclusions against what goes on out there in that same world where research subjects are doing the things that the science claims to be about. This is neither radical nor is it rocket science. It is nothing more than a requirement that a science closely engage its phenomenon of interest.

But enough with the Mill-bashing. As I used to tell students, it's not nice to stand on the shoulders of giants and then spend all your time whacking them on the head with a rolled-up term paper. Returning to the works of the master helps see BSS and HSR and their differences more clearly. And, in spite of the differences, Mill's inductive logic remains a masterpiece, a work of genius to guide critical thought, scientist or not. Pay attention. Look for things that co-occur. Don't get carried away. Look for cases where they don't co-occur. Expect to be wrong and treat the negative results as an opportunity to learn more.

Mill requires us to seek out *negative cases*, cases that don't fit, and we have to look for them in some systematic way on a continual basis as part of any research project. This is the simple down-to-earth meaning of *falsification* as one requirement for any science, BSS or HSR or any other variation on the theme. The trick here, the way to shift the logic from BSS to HSR, is to do Mill's "inducing" as an ongoing process in the real human social world rather than using his logic as a justification to oversimplify and reduce that world to a caricature of its usual self.

In a later chapter, inductive logic will be planted in a more dynamic and layered research approach. Induction as a concept will not only remain central; it will be one of the primary engines that propel a research project along its path. The logic siblings, inductive and deductive, will grow into a much larger family that includes some eccentric relatives as well. And of course there will always be a place for a conversation between HSR and a BSS laboratory moment, as this book will show, but BSS will be a shot of espresso in an airport coffee shop between flights, not the whole trip or the home airport or the final destination.

There is still a problem here, though, that nonlinearity alone doesn't handle, the problem for the next chapter. Theories of complexity and chaos help tremendously with HSR epistemology. But that new nonlinear science, like the old one, arose in non-human research worlds. As the new science diffused into human social science, jargon appeared that used a "physics" suffix, as in "econophysics," and "sociophysics." Complexity slid right back into the famous saying of Rutherford, cited earlier, that all science in the end reduces to physics.

The problem was, and is, that this epistemological move ignores the most important characteristics of the phenomenon of human social science, namely, humans living in their social world. So, once again, we have to rescue human social science from the clutches of "all science is physics," while using the insights of complexity and chaos that much of contemporary physics also supports. It is the unique characteristics of human social worlds that make HSR a truly different kind of science. That topic is where we'll go in the next chapter.

An HSR Parable

Maybe a good way to end this chapter is with a story.

In my teaching days it used to depress me, the BSS students who would traipse through my office looking for someone to care about their HSR insights. As "qualitative" research became more popular through the 1980s and the 1990s, grad students from BSS disciplines, which were all of them but anthropology at the University of Maryland, would show up at my door. Here's a hypothetical example of what would happen.

A student from a BSS department walks in, looks around nervously, and says in a quiet voice. "I'm working on my dissertation and I've got a problem. I'm supposed to do a linear regression to explain this dependent variable. But…"And with that the student pulls out a piece of paper with stains made of equal parts of tears and pizza grease. A diagram shows a large number of tiny boxes. The boxes are filled with all manner of things that the student knows are relevant to what he is trying to understand. Some of the things happen at the same time, some of them happen one after another. Arrows fill the spaces between the boxes, and sometimes they make loops. It looks like spiders of different sizes pressed flat on the paper. "Can you help me with this?" asks the student. "No," I say, or finally learned to say with experience.

I tell them to go back to their department and never talk to anyone like me again until their dissertation is signed. The HSR way will bring madness and possible career death to vulnerable BSS grad students. And not just madness. It will make a mess of their exams, annoy their faculty, and someone like me as the outside member of their five person committee won't be able to prevent the carnage. I tried a couple of times and in the end my only option was to drug the committee and order rendition to Napoleon's old prison on Corsica. Writing a dissertation is as much, if not more, a political act as it is a scholarly one. Ask Foucault, who had a great deal to say about the relation between knowledge and power.

But the truth is, the interest of those students who came through my office door in increasing numbers——their interest in patterns in a human social world, the many links among many different things, how they unfold over time in the experience of the people in whom they are interested——this is exactly what an HSR researcher aspires to, and this is exactly the kind of science I mean to describe in this book. Mill knew the limits. He wrote:

> For even if we could try experiments upon a nation or upon the human race, with as little scruple as M. Majendie tries them upon dogs or rabbits, we should never succeed in making two instances identical in every respect except the presence or absence of some one indefinite circumstance (pg. 360).

And, as he notices in passing, it gets even worse, because human social causes themselves are "in a state of perpetual alteration."

Mill was his own best critic, adding "intellectual integrity" to the long list of reasons to admire him. But in the end he sculpted a version of human social science out of Enlightenment natural science that limited, even distorted, the representation of the phenomenon that the science was about. In the next chapter we turn to two major figures, one of whom admired Mill, one of whom thought he completely missed the point. They started the modern counterargument, the one that this book also represents, that human social science was—and still is—a different breed of research cat.

CHAPTER THREE

The Road to HSR Is Paved with Everyday Intentions

John Stuart Mill, looking back from today, stands out as a, if not the, major figure that shaped the modern extension of "science" into the human social world. He succeeded in part because of his genius, but he also had the wind of the previous century's science at his back. He is a poster child for what is usually called Anglo-American empiricism. I used him in the previous chapter, not only to show the roots of BSS, but also because he is very clear, and refreshingly self-critical, when he lays out the limitations of his logic. Those limitations lead straight to HSR.

The Anglo-American tradition wasn't the only 19th century game in town, though the others tended to be played across the English Channel. Foundations for a different way of thinking about human social science brewed in several countries, especially in Germany, based on the work of Kant and Hegel. I decided to focus on two of the giants who followed them. I will write about them here more briefly than I did about Mill in the previous chapter, because the concepts they introduce will thread through the rest of this book. Here I just want to acknowledge the pioneers and show how they rebuilt the Enlightenment science bandwagon.

The German-language sources make biographical sense for me, since I've lived and worked in Austria many times over the years. Besides, my original training was in linguistic and cultural anthropology, and as a reader has already seen and will see again, my favorite BSS-type discipline is social psychology, now morphed into "social cognition" after it climbed onto the coattails of the "cognitive science" revolution. In the U.S., both those fields are linked with German and Austrian figures, immigrants like Franz Boas for anthropology and Kurt Lewin for social psychology. My biases run in a Teutonic direction.

I'll focus here on Franz Brentano and Wilhelm Dilthey. Both discuss John Stuart Mill's work, Brentano favorably. But then Brentano, with his concept of "intentionality," brought up the inconvenient fact that the "objects" of human social science, unlike gas molecules, are also "subjects." And, worse yet, so are the researchers. Everyone involved in the human social science business has beliefs, desires and emotions, said Brentano. Dilthey went even further and said that Mill, and natural science, pretty much missed the point completely, because they ignored human history as it was lived in everyday experience. In a nutshell, they both said, fundamental characteristics of the phenomenon of human social science are missing in Mill's formulation. BSS might be a science, but what is it a science *of?*

I wondered if anyone else had picked the two, Brentano and Dilthey, and featured them as a natural pair to excavate the fundamentals of HSR. When I was in graduate school, we didn't learn much about either of them. It turns out I'm not the only one to match them up, though there don't appear to be many of us. Marias wrote in his history of philosophy that the two of them "essentially complement one another, and it is not difficult to see how the philosophy of our time derives from their joint influence." And writing about the Spanish philosopher Ortega y Gasset, Graham says that he "linked himself mentally with the generation of Brentano and Dilthey…"

I'll start this chapter with Brentano. He left us with ambiguous messages that have kept debates going to this day. There is an entire German language journal called *Brentano Studien*. Peter Simons, the translator of his book, *Psychology from an Empirical Standpoint*, describes the eternal debate over his core concept, *intentionality*: "Few passages have been pored over so intensively as this, and few have given rise to such heated controversy" (pg. xviii—page numbers in this section refer to Brentano's book cited in the notes). Let's take a look at this concept of intentionality, a concept that alerts us to how research subjects are making sense out of things in ways that researchers probably don't suspect is going on. Subjects, as it turns out, have minds of their own.

A Fallen Jesuit

Franz Brentano (1838-1917) read John Stuart Mill and liked much of what he had to say. He argued in his own book, published in 1874, that there was no reason why human social research couldn't be as systematic and precise as the natural sciences. He sounds, on the face of it, like yet another in a long line of early Mill-like cheerleaders.

But he threw the developing BSS world a curve. Some idea of its power can be seen with a list of his students, people like Edmund Husserl, a founder of phenomenology, and Sigmund Freud, founder of psychiatry. Brentano wanted psychology to be an *empirical* science, based on direct personal experience with the phenomenon of interest. But—here comes the curve—what was the phenomenon of interest? Some of it involved *events in the mind*. Psychology didn't reduce down to nerves firing with sensations and telling muscles what to do. Minds held beliefs and desires and emotions that changed from mind to mind and from time to time and therefore changed what people thought and what they did as a result. The *objects* of research are also *subjects*.

With mind in the picture, how could psychology be empirical? A long discussion ensues in his book that need not detain us here. But one obvious solution was, psychologists had access to their own mind. They couldn't really observe it as it did its work, because as soon as the observation started, attention shifted and the work stopped. But they could access it though memory and get some inkling of what had been going on.

A descriptive psychology, as Brentano called it, had to take some of its data from a *first person point of view*. A psychologist would have to look within herself to investigate the mind and how it worked. Where else was she supposed to look to get any empirical data? This suggestion is at odds with the usual scientific notion of "objectivity," to put it mildly. Traditional science says that the scientist should have no influence over the research. That would be "subjective." The problem is, the scientist is, in fact, a "subject," and therefore a legitimate part of the data.

Even physicists now think the old-fashioned notion of objectivity is nuts, but in ancient times, when I was a graduate student, the "researcher disappearing act" was even reflected in the rules for writing an article. Never, but never, was a researcher to use the first-person pronoun. "I" was simply not there. A researcher was only a passive instrument, in the passive voice, a facilitator of the interaction between disembodied method and objective reality, replaceable by any other scientist who was trained in how *not* to be there, too.

But if a principal source of data is what's going on in the mind, the mind of the research subject and the mind of the researcher, as Brentano argued, we've landed in a BSS oxymoron. The phrase "first person objective science" is not a possible concept. Brentano acknowledged that "third person objective" psychology was also a reasonable thing to do, and he supported it. He called it "genetic psychology," a type of psychology that foreshadowed behaviorism. But that's not really what interested him. He was after consciousness, and consciousness did its work in our heads, so our heads had to be a source of data.

It was confusing, this curve that Brentano threw. He came by his confusion honestly, though. He became a Jesuit priest, then left the order because he couldn't accept the doctrine of the Pope's infallibility. As a recovering Catholic myself, I know the problem. Then he became a Viennese professor, but he had to leave Austria because they wouldn't let former priests get married and he was in love with the provocatively named Ida von Lieben, "Liebe" meaning "love" in German. Then he returned to Austria, but they wouldn't give him his job back, so he left again. He wrote articles for a Viennese newspaper called "My Last Wishes for Austria." I was an exchange student and a visiting professor many times in Austria, so I understand that, too.

With this kind of biography it's not hard to see why Brentano argued that mental and physical phenomena just aren't the same kind of thing. You can't *reduce* (that John Stuart Mill word again) the one to the other. Psychology is not all physiology, though he of course couldn't have anticipated how much more interesting that question would become today with contemporary research in fields like cognitive neuroscience.

The important point for the moment is that Brentano was one of the early figures in Western human social science that took exception to the idea that it and the natural sciences should be lumped together in the same category. Brentano still wanted research on humans to be pursued in a scientific way. But he complicated things considerably when he argued that the mental part of the science can never be done adequately only from an *outsider's third person point of view*. His premise became HSR's premise. You can't do a science of human subjects unless you investigate *their* first person point of view. And you can't avoid the fact that *your* first person point of view is part of the science as well.

Intentionality

Researcher and researched are both human. Both have minds that make them different from rocks and trees and frogs. A human social science can't describe and explain the mental life of human subjects just by observing motion of their bodies through space and time. It has to get inside, into the mind, into the first-person perspective. And researchers, being human as well, know something about how that first-person perspective works, because they have one as well.

The concept Brentano created to describe this first-person viewpoint, the famous one that everyone quotes to this day, is "intentionality." Here is one often-cited version of what he means by that term, one of the many quotes he produced that feeds the ongoing Brentano interpretation industry:

> Every mental phenomenon is characterized by what the Scholastics of the Middle Ages called the intentional (or mental) inexistence of an object, and what we might call, though not wholly unambiguously, reference to a content, direction toward an object (which is not to be understood

here as meaning a thing), or immanent objectivity. Every mental phenomenon includes something as object within itself... (Pg. 88).

That word salad makes you yearn for Mill's clear and crisp definition of inductive logic, doesn't it? We're not the only ones to react that way. Platoons of acolytes have devoted their careers to what Brentano actually meant. It apparently annoyed him when his followers did so. Maybe he considered it all perfectly clear. An ex-Jesuit in love with von Lieben living in exile in Florence might have seen things differently. But then that was one of the points he was making.

There's an aside worth mentioning here. Human social science is stereotyped as the land of fuzzy concepts and fuzzier minds, with hydra-headed jargon lurking in the shadows that will paralyze you with the poison of vagueness and ambiguity before you even have a chance to try and figure out what in the hell they might mean. It's not only Brentano. The "culture" concept from anthropology, for instance, is now used in so many different ways in so many different applications that it's not clear what *it* means anymore.

The stereotype has some truth to it. But in part—only in part—the word salad is excusable. The real world, filled as it is with variable human intentionalities, is messy. It made John Stuart Mill a little crazy when he wrote about it. It reminds me of what I think of as Einstein's paradox. He actually said this. "As far as the laws of mathematics refer to reality, they are not certain; and as far as they are certain, they do not refer to reality." If the phenomena are messy, so will be their representation in the language of science, however noble is the scientist's struggles to be precise. Ambiguity and vagueness are characteristics of the phenomenon. Without those characteristics, the human social world would implode.

But really, Brentano is a little over the top. Dilthey is even worse. So let me use a clearer definition of intentionality from my computer dictionary. It's against academic rules to use an ordinary dictionary, but I left the university in the mid-90s, so I can now look things up in normal places like sane people do. My computer dictionary says that, in philosophy, "intentionality" means:

> the quality of mental states (e.g., thoughts, beliefs, desires, hopes) that consists in their being directed toward some object or state of affairs.

A little better. At a conference I attended years ago, I asked a drunken phenomenologist, "What in the @#$% is intentionality anyway?" Phenomenology grew right out of Brentano and took his concept of intentionality with it, so it was a fair question. He answered without hesitation: "Consciousness has an object, and right now my consciousness has as its object another beer." That I understood, as well as its inverse, that a beer might be many different things to different people with their different consciousness of the moment.

For humans, there is no world separate from mind, and there is no mind separate from world. All due respect to the Buddha. The bond between the two comes with the human subject territory. It is like a chemical bond between hydrogen and oxygen that produces water, the very part/whole problem that John Stuart Mill wanted to keep at arm's length as part of his science. Intentionality is part of being human, so it has to be part of human social science. HSR has to deal with this object/consciousness blend, and that means it has to get at subject first person perspectives.

Intention and Purpose

Intentionality is a foundation stone for HSR. Human social science—or any science of sentient beings for that matter—has to be different because of it. Descriptions and explanations of human social worlds involve "subjective" mental states, period. First-person viewpoints must be part of the data and part of the explanation. Both subjects and researchers behave, in part, in terms of all those beliefs and desires and emotions and purposes in their intentional state of the moment.

Why did the human subject cross the road? Because he had the *belief* that the approaching street sweeper was about to spray him when it went by and he had a *desire* to stay dry. And why did the researcher write that in her notebook? Because she had the *belief* that it would add to her work on the sociology of urban life and she had a *desire* to publish an article.

Before putting Brentano's concept to work, though, one important argument within the ranks of the intentional horde deserves some comment. Brentano, and many who came later, tell you that intentionality isn't the same as "intention," at least as most of us think about it. Most of us think about "intention" meaning "for some purpose." Brentano gets away with this argument by saying you can get "purpose" from "desire." If you desire something, you set out to get it, and that becomes your purpose.

Things can get convoluted in ways we don't need here. For now, let me just say that Kant had already laid out a version of the elements of intentionality, namely, *cognition, feeling* and *will* (pg. 182). The three are independent of each other, he said, but they blend together into the famous "unity of consciousness" at any given moment, a concept that foreshadows the development of modern ideas like "schema" and "mental model." For instance, you can know about something, like my adolescent dream of a Corvette, feel strongly that you want it, and go out and rob a bank to pay for it, all in the same coherent intentional package.

Arguments over what the ground floor of intentionality might look like are interesting, but I don't want to get lost in debates that have been going on for a couple of centuries that I don't need for my purposes here. At the same time, it seems clear that human will, or purpose, or goal, has to be part of any human social world that HSR sets out to research and describe and explain. It's not all beliefs and desires and feelings. A first-person perspective means that one is doing *something with reference to some outcome.* I admit, the purpose of faculty meetings was a challenge to understand when I was a professor. Even there, though, some colleagues looked forward to them, "looking forward" being the purposive point.

Remember the Subaru Forester example I used in the discussion of John Stuart Mill? Remember the problems with "cause?" I didn't buy that particular vehicle so much because any particular thing *caused* me to. I mostly bought it because I wanted to *do* something with it. I *intended* to drive on muddy or snow-covered roads in the country, for example. The car had all wheel drive, which would make that easier to do. And it had a compass to keep track of where I was on the networks of unmarked dirt roads in the mountains. I could stare at it as I drove off a cliff.

Purpose, goals, some point to it all—they have to be a part of intentionality as well. Fortunately I can skip to the present and draw on a contemporary, one who is much clearer on the concept, a person known for his work in artificial intelligence. Like human social scientists, the artificial intelligentsia want to explain a system that is *doing* something. In their case, it's a computer whose beliefs and desires and goals are coded into a program. Daniel Dennett, in his 1989 book *The Intentional Stance*, takes Brentano and stirs in some computer science:

> Here is how it works: first you decide to treat the object whose behavior is to be predicted as a rational agent; then you figure out what beliefs that agent ought to have, given its place in the world and its purpose. Then you figure out what desires it ought to have, on the same considerations, and finally you predict that this rational agent will act to further its goals in the light of its beliefs. A little practical reasoning from the chosen set of beliefs and desires will in most instances yield a decision about what the agent ought to do; that is what you predict the agent will do.

There were problems in the preceding chapter and there will be more to come with concepts like "prediction" and "rationality," but ignore them for the moment. We'll get to them soon. Dennett's not bad for a computer science type. And for the moment, notice how he uses intentionality to figure out what a system is *doing*. That's what we're going to do in this book, only with humans instead of computers.

What it all boils down to is that any science of humans in their social world must describe and explain their intentional stance. Intentionality cannot be explained only from what you see on the surface from your third-person point of view. A researcher has to ask, "What are they thinking? What are they feeling? What are they doing? What are they after?" A scientist has to be able to answer those questions, just like ordinary humans do in their everyday life when they're trying to understand what another person is up to. The problem is, the researcher has to answer in a *scientific* way and include her own intentions in the bargain. That is *the* problem for HSR that we need to solve in this book. In the next chapter, building an intentional description of people who will never be completely aware of their own intentionality will become a full-time job.

Research Handles to Get a Grip on Intentions

Say we're HSR researchers and we launch into a project. We know we have to learn and describe research subject intentionality. All well and good. But what do we claim that the descriptions we come up with represent? Brentano talks about *consciousness* and *desire* leading to *purpose*. Dennett talks about *rationality*. Do we really want to claim that a description of research subject intentionality can be determined from what those subjects *consciously* and *rationally* think as they go about their business?

God forbid. There is a clinical diagnosis for those who think humans are always and only conscious and rational. That diagnosis is "terminal denial." A model of humans as conscious and rational flies in the face of some of the most interesting work going on now. Are we rational? In previous chapters a few of the many "cognitive biases" humans have were mentioned, including the decades old work on cognitive dissonance. And are we fully conscious? Brentano's student Freud drove that train out of the station in the early 20th century. Why did the patient complain that her arm was paralyzed from the shoulder down? There is no way that an "arm" can be paralyzed as a unit that starts neatly at the shoulder joint and runs all the way down to the fingertips. On the other hand, an "arm" is a mental unit of the body for most people. The patient's mind paralyzed her "arm," the anatomical unit real to her unconscious.

A less dramatic everyday problem for the conscious rational mind is *habit*. Habits might start with rational conscious experience, say when a person first learns to do something. But then once learned, the skill become an automatic pattern that the learner isn't aware of anymore. It isn't conscious, and it isn't rational. A person doesn't stop and think about how best to achieve his goal. He just does what he has always done in that situation. It saves a lot of time and energy, but what happens if the situation changes? Then that same useful pattern can turn into an ossified maladaptive routine.

For example, driving a car is pretty complicated when you first learn. It wasn't hard for me, since I grew up in California and read *Hot Rod* magazine and biographies of racecar drivers. I'd been driving in my mind long before I got behind the wheel. But then driving *habits* can turn on you later if the world changes and you don't. There was a day when seatbelts did not exist. When they first appeared, even after they were required by law, I refused to wear them. I wasn't the only one. I won't go into all the pathologies that might explain why. I will just say that something finally snapped, probably old age, and I realized how stupid I was being and now I wear them all the time. Now seat belts are a habit.

Snapping on a seat belt is no more a conscious and rational act now than downshifting when I want to slow down. It is out-of-awareness and habitual, not conscious and rational. So is much of life for research subjects. And researchers. Describing and explaining human social life has to take into account the beliefs and desires and feelings and purposes of those humans, where that intentionality came from, and how it shapes the experiences that they have. HSR has to include it, whether it is conscious and rational or not, and more often than not, "not" is what we're dealing with.

Rational Reconstruction

Now what? How are we supposed to describe the non-conscious and non-rational intentionality of research subjects?

The description is something we *make up*, then *test*, then *revise*, and then *test* again. The researcher builds a *model*, a model of what a person who "acts like that" might believe and desire and feel and be trying to do. The description can be based on observation, or on what a subject says, on imagination, or on empathy, or on god knows what else in who knows what kinds of combination. What matters is that a researcher makes her claim about subject intentionality clear, tests it out, and then stands ready to revise it and test it again until the description works.

What is this? Science fiction? No, it is a strategy that points right at HSR science, but the story of that different science has only just begun. Making up and testing out a model of intentionality is to HSR what a hypothesis is to BSS. As you'll see in the next chapter, it even involves Mill's inductive logic, among other things. As the statistician with the great name of George Box said, all models are wrong, but some models are useful.

There is a smorgasbord of good brain food for making up wrong and useful models of intentionality. Here is a sample. Alfred Schütz, another Austrian immigrant to the U.S., talked about how a researcher had to imagine *in-order-to* and *because* motives to describe what research subjects were up to. And George Kelly, an American psychologist, described an *as if* approach. Think about describing something "as if" some intentional stance were in operation, he said. (But it must be added that a German, Hans Valhinger, inspired him). The sociologist Max Weber, another German more likely to be known to readers who have taken a sociology course, offers a concept of *social action* that includes intentionality, not to mention an entire sociology characterized as "anti-positivism." And Edith Stein, a student of Husserl's who appears in the last chapter of this book, directs the self-absorbed intentional musings of Brentano outward into the world of others.

The main question for now is, how can a researcher "make something up" that feeds into HSR as a science? Making up a description of intentionality has to aim eventually at evidence, logic and falsification.

In fact, people make up models of other peoples' intentionality all the time in ordinary life. It comes to us as naturally as does induction. It's how we evolved. The danger lies in how often it is done in oversimplified and self-serving ways, at its worst in the form of racism and many other -isms in service of preconceived notions and emotionally loaded habits. He did *what*? Well, what would you expect from someone who would buy a Subaru.

HSR serves as an antidote to such oversimplified caricatures. There is work to do for the rest of this book to justify the claim that a useful but dangerous human ability can be turned into a science, but with any luck by the end it will make sense. It's not so different from what Mill had to do with induction, take a natural ability and build it into a science so that it could be used to understand and explain a human social world without distorting it to fit a person's prior beliefs.

My favorite framework for "making things up" to describe research subject intentionality comes from another German, sociologist Jürgen Habermas, another intellectual giant, still with us, whose work spans several disciplines and several decades.

HSR is what Habermas calls a *reconstructive science*. The phrase sounds like a training course for dentists or plastic surgeons. A better comparison would be sciences like geology or astronomy, or humanities like history, or jobs like that of the TV detective Colombo. HSR, like those examples, takes evidence that is already out there in the world and organizes a plausible description and explanation based on it. The science "reconstructs" something that already happened based on the evidence it leaves behind. Then that reconstruction, in turn, becomes a hypothesis to test against new data, all the while following Mill's advice to find negative examples that complicate and contradict it.

In HSR, the reconstruction focuses on making sense of what other people do in terms of their intentionality. The model that a researcher makes up is what he calls a *rational reconstruction*. Be careful with those words, though. It is *not* rational because a researcher assumes that the subject acts rationally. It is called rational because a scientist creates it in the detached scientific mode of evidence-logic-falsification. And it is *not* conscious because a researcher assumes that it models what a person actually thinks about as they do something. It is conscious because a researcher *self-consciously* constructs and presents it. A rational reconstruction is a researcher's job, an explicit model to challenge in the test-modify-retest cycles of HSR methodologies.

A rational reconstruction shows an outsider how to understand who the research subjects are and what they are doing. It helps outsiders make sense of things. It is more a *translation* between subject first person view and audience third person view than anything else, a way of thinking about HSR that will take up the better part of Chapter Six.

A researcher also uses rational reconstruction to try out what she thinks she knows about subjects with the subjects themselves. To tell the truth, some of the more interesting moments in HSR, in my experience, come when a researcher shows subjects how the researcher thinks that the subjects think when they're doing something that they're not thinking about. It's never a neutral reaction. It runs from "aha" to "bullshit," and, wherever it falls along the scale, from epiphany to annoyance, it always adds new data to the mix that drives the research forward to places it never knew existed when it first started. From a research subject's point of view, it sometimes produces a self- awareness in a way that resembles counseling more than data collection. I don't think I've ever seen that discussed in the professional human social science literature. Probably the question is too "cognitively dissonant" with delusions of objectivity.

An Example

Here's a brief example of how this rational reconstruction business works in practice. When I lived in Austria, the country that wouldn't let Brentano the married ex-priest have his job back, I spent some time making sense of an Austrian concept called "Schmäh." It's a long story that a reader can find elsewhere if they're interested, but here's the short version.

I *reconstructed* the concept *rationally*. It was a lot of work and involved every method, non-method, intuition and hallucination in the HSR toolbox. There was no simple definition and sometimes people told me there was no definition at all. In quick summary, the reconstruction went like this: A fundamental part of Schmäh-like talking or acting is that it is based on *irony*. Specifically, things aren't what they seem; they're actually much worse; but there's no point in getting upset about it. Laugh it off.

A sample of Schmäh: There is a joke about Germans that Austrians tell. It has a lot of different set-ups, but the punch line is the same. The German says, "The situation is serious but not hopeless." The Austrian replies, "No, the situation is hopeless but not serious."

In my rational reconstruction, Schmäh turned out to be a general attitude towards life that bubbled up into many of its moments. As far as whether the use of Schmäh was *conscious*, it never occurred to me to claim that any Austrian consciously thought "Schmäh = irony." Most of the time when I proposed my reconstruction to Austrians, I got a laugh and an "aha" reaction, an important indication that I was onto something that they knew but didn't know they knew. Nor did I ever think some kind of "irony rule" was involved in order to rationally calculate whether someone would perform a Schmäh or not. Maybe some thought that way once in awhile, maybe they didn't, sometimes, never or always. It didn't matter for the rational reconstruction of their intentionality. What mattered was that the reconstruction made it possible for outsiders—me and my audience—to see and understand and learn how to interpret and respond to it.

The science part came in when I looked at how the rational reconstruction worked, and how it didn't, in different situations, including as always John Stuart Mill's search for negative cases. I could easily have constructed some pseudo-experiments, though I didn't do that. Hundreds of pieces of data were already available, from written material, conversations, experiences, stories, informal interviews, observations, all the usual kinds of material that the world provides that then have to be organized into a systematic form. In one class I taught in Vienna we did a survey and informal interviews to test the reconstruction as well. A lot of Austrians—including academic colleagues—got a kick out of my work because it rang true even though they'd never consciously thought about Schmäh. And then of course my own ability to understand and do Schmäh improved considerably because I was learning to use it even as I researched it.

One of my favorite moments was a conference with professional colleagues where I first presented the Schmäh rational reconstruction in an academic context. As far as I was concerned, it was a chance for more data collection. A senior colleague known for conference naps remained wide awake and laughed all the way through it. Another got up to give his talk, looked at me and grinned, and said "Was that about Schmäh or was it an example of it?" The conference was the sort of validation of HSR work that usually doesn't get reported. If you can make a critical academic audience of native-speaker linguists aware of a central concept in their language in a new way that makes sense to them, you must be onto something.

The point is that a rational reconstruction of intentionality, even though a researcher makes it up, leads right *into* science, not *away* from it. An HSR researcher doesn't have to claim that it represents anything other than his or her hard work to learn, test and make clear how a third-person outsider can understand a first-person insider's intentionality, an intentionality that the insider might not even be able to describe. To use a phrase from a famous book by Michael Polanyi, the HSR job is to make a model of *tacit knowledge* (not to mention desires and emotions and purposes) explicit. That's all HSR is required to claim. It can claim more if it wants to and is willing to do the extra work, but it's not necessary to get on with the job.

Habermas gives us more than just rational reconstruction, though. Intentionality is also a *human universal*. How it works, what makes it possible, and how it is that humans have intentionality at all—these are general questions worthy of a fundamental theory of what it means to be human. As Habermas put it, writing "pre-theoretical knowledge" where I'd say "tacit":

> When the pre-theoretical knowledge to be reconstructed expresses a universal capability, a general cognitive, linguistic, or interactive competence (or sub-competence), then what begins as an explication of meaning aims at the reconstruction of species competencies.

Building a rational reconstruction, Habermas says, is also *theory building* of a type different from what BSS usually means by that phrase. Creating rational reconstructions isn't just a way to think about HSR in the context of a particular project. It is also a way to think about a theory of what it means to be human, a noble calling that will receive more attention in Chapter Six.

Anglos and Saxons

There is another story to tell here, a sidebar for this book, a story alive today in everything from serious debate to wisecracks based on stereotypes. According to the stereotype, the English and the Americans are the source of BSS. The Germans have the elaborate track record in HSR. It's kind of true. The national origin of different kinds of human social science really does make for a good conversation. It's worth a lot more attention than it is getting here.

One year when I was working at the University of Vienna, a German professor and I, the two opening speakers at a conference, were getting ready to perform cultural theater for an Austrian audience. Our Austrian colleague came in and told a joke. Right before a lecture, she said, a German speaker walked in with an armful of books, dripping with bookmarks showing the important passages, all from a multi-volume set called *Introduction to Elephant Science*. An American walked in with a one-page handout called *How to Use an Elephant.* We both laughed. I'm laughing now. That's exactly what I'm trying to do with Brentano and Dilthey, to go from elephant science to how to ride one. Remember the joke about Schmäh I quoted earlier in this section? For our Austrian colleague, right before the conference, the situation was hopeless but not serious.

This isn't the time or place to untangle the complicated winding and twisting history of BSS and HSR in a sort of massive *War and Peace* way. Besides, readers who favor other national traditions of human social science are already spitting mad at the neglect of their favorites. I can especially hear screams of Gallic outrage as I write this book. But it is interesting how, when it comes to building HSR from the ground up, German intellectual history contains so much of the useful material, at least from my point of view. It's probably no accident that "theoretically grounded concept" is a cliché phrase in academic German conversations.

German/Austrian or English/American, in the end, a different version of human social science has been around for the better part of two centuries. Brentano threw a first-person curve into John Stuart Mill's science. The next 19th century figure I want to look at, Wilhelm Dilthey, threw an HSR screwball, beat it to the plate, and then hit it out of the park. He elaborated on what an intentional system might mean in living color and aimed the science squarely at what people were doing in their own worlds in their own time. Mill was no role-model for him.

The Birth of the Human Sciences

Wilhelm Dilthey (1833-1911) is the third 19th century pioneer consulted in this book. No more wishy-washy hybrid HSR/BSS with him. He threw open a window and looked out on what HSR needed to become. Then he threw open another window. He kept throwing windows open until the day he died. His translator, who obviously admires his work, put it this way: He jumped on his horse and rode off in all directions. Dilthey himself regretted at the end that he'd never finished the job he set out to do.

He used a vocabulary fuzzier than Brentano's and went through several versions of his ideas during his life. Apparently he was a pretty boring German professor, though he was good at it, since he wound up in Hegel's academic chair. Important a figure as he is for HSR, I wanted him to have been more dramatic, like Van Gogh or something, maybe cutting off his ear at a John Stuart Mill lecture.

Even though he pales compared with the colorful Brentano, he was one of the first who could talk the HSR talk and walk the HSR walk. Dilthey read Mill and, unlike Brentano, thought Mill had pretty much missed the point. He also read Husserl, Brentano's student who founded phenomenology, and brought intentionality into his own work. But then he said the phenomenologists missed the point, too, when they claimed the ultimate answer was an eternal and universal world out there that you could think your way into.

Most important of all, Dilthey thought that the natural sciences, "Naturwissenschaften" in German, really missed the point when they claimed authority over what all of science should look like. He was bothered like I'm bothered, and like I hope a reader of this book is bothered by now. Human social science seemed hollow, lifeless, when humans were boxed into a natural science way of researching. It just didn't get at the subjects' real world, in living color, over time, the very phenomenon that the science is, in the end, supposed to be about. Dilthey's translator sums him up by saying that his focus on the combination of *actual human life* and *history,* both at the same time, is what made him the important figure that he is. The "actual human life" part is obvious. History, for him, meant that humans are "evolutionary and developmental beings" with intentions and purposes that change over time (pg. 15—page references in this section refer to Dilthey's book, cited in the chapter notes).

Dilthey was still after a science, though it was going to have to be different from the version that was then—and still is—dominant. But what specific kinds of research should he say that this new science included? Why wasn't there a general name for all the approaches that shared this focus on human social worlds? The fact that there wasn't such a name—still isn't for the most part, which is why I had to make up "HSR" to write this book—tells you something about the enduring Newtonian influence. Dilthey created a famous label to cover them all, "Geisteswissenschaften" in the German plural. Well, it's famous if you took a course in sociology and learned it from the writings of Max Weber.

This stereotypically German-sounding word doesn't translate directly into "human social research." "Geist" orbits around meanings of "spirit" and "mind" and "intellect," among other things, and "Wissenschaft" moves in the direction of "science" but also comes from "Wissen" or "knowledge." "Geisteswissenschaft" is sometimes translated as "the humanities."

But it is clear that Dilthey's goal is also my goal, and the goal of all of us who followed him. He wanted an alternative to the natural sciences to better guide research that focused on humans, so I'll go ahead and use my term, HSR, for what he called Geisteswissenschaft. As we used to say in Washington, "close enough for government work," though the way things have gone with government recently, that's not as reassuring as it used to be, and it wasn't all that reassuring even back in the days when I lived there.

The Dismal BSS Sciences

So what's wrong with human social research based on the natural sciences? What was Dilthey's problem? What's missing when it is extended to cover humans in society? Oh, Dilthey said, just *life* itself, life as lived out there in the world by the humans Dilthey wanted to build a science of. The stripped-down cartoon figures of humans with their abstract minds and their deductive/inductive reasoning—those images weren't what an HSR should be about if it meant to be about real people living real lives.

> There is no real blood flowing in the veins of the knowing subject fabricated by Locke, Hume, and Kant, but only the diluted juice of reason as mere mental activity. But dealing with the whole man in history and psychology led me to take the whole man—in the multiplicity of his powers; this willing-feeling-perceiving being—as the basis for explaining knowledge and its concepts (pg. 73).

Dilthey's rant should sound familiar by now. It's a theme of this book. When he talks about "the growing power of the natural sciences," he adds:

> The answers of Comte and the positivists as well as John Stuart Mill and the empiricists to these questions seemed to me to mutilate historical reality to accommodate concepts and methods of the natural sciences (pg. 72).

My hero.

Here is another word to add to your German vocabulary.

"Erlebnis." It is based on "Leben" or "life," and it translates as "experience," though in my Austrian youth it also had overtones of "adventure," like it does in English. Erlebnis was translated into academic English as *lived experience,* and that phrase is alive and well as jargon in English-language HSR today. Erlebnis, was the heart, the principal focus, of Dilthey's new human social science.

What does Erlebnis mean exactly? It's best not to look too closely. Like most of the core terms that Dilthey uses, it slips and slides like a greyhound on a frozen lake. In a general way, though, it's pretty clear what he's getting at. If you think in terms of people actually doing things, it's not so far away from Brentano's shift from "third person" to "first person" psychology, only it's "first person life" as well as "first person mind."

For that matter, it's like the famous quote from Bronislaw Malinowski, an early 20th century anthropologist. We learned to chant his words in graduate school in our quaint neocolonial way. The point of our research, said Malinowski, was "to grasp the native's point of view, his relation to life, to realize his vision of his world." Malinowski is considered to be the father of the famous *participant observation*, the call to get out of the lab and into the world of people in whom you are interested.

Much of what HSR is about, much of what Dilthey and Brentano were after—I think it's all about this *point of view shift.* To do HSR, a scientist has to first learn how to adapt his or her habitual point of view to an understanding of how a different subject point of view works. And, since that point of view is not something a research subject can usually describe, using researcher concepts, on demand, in twenty-five words or less, I think Dilthey is saying you've got to infer it from the subject's lived experience—in other words, *make up an evidence-based rational reconstruction that shows how subject intentionality is part of a larger lived experience pattern.*

A point of view, at any particular moment, consists of an intentional stance in some lived experience context. An individual's intentionality is shaped by biography and circumstances, in a world of limits set by culture and society and political economy and environment. No a priori abstract framework—"metaphysics," Dilthey called it—could ever handle such complicated moments. But if that's all true, then how are we supposed to make a science out of the Geisteswissenschaften? If it's all so complicated and specific to the lived experience of the moment, how does a researcher handle it? Maybe it's just too rich, intricate, and of the moment to ever do anything but dive in, say "oh wow," and go home?

This is the slippery slope called "historicism," what we would more likely call "relativism" today. The argument, carried to extremes, is that everything, everyone, every moment is unique, something to be learned and appreciated only in its own specific terms. No generalization would ever be possible. Neither Dilthey nor this book makes that insane argument, though Dilthey was accused of it. True enough, generalization is never easy in HSR. Of course it isn't so easy in BSS, either, if you recall the quote about "ecological validity" in the previous chapter. That quote defined the term as meaning that tight laboratory control made it difficult if not impossible to generalize study results to what people did in real life.

You know the New Age cliché, "today is the first day of the rest of your life," a quote attributed to the founder of Synanon, ironically enough given my years of drug research? Well, "this paragraph is the beginning of the rest of the book." We have a general picture of what we need for HSR and what it means to report it in a scientific way. Now we need to think about how to get there from here. I want to start by untangling that complicated lived experience and intentionality that a researcher must investigate, learn, document, and then represent in rational reconstructions. With a little clarity on lived experience we can get to the next chapter and build a logic to help get the research done without collapsing into tearful paralysis at the unbearable uniqueness and complexity of every moment of life. (That sentence, by the way, is a Schmäh).

Same, Different, and a Little of Both

HSR, Dilthey said, is a science of lived experience. And the science, like Habermas said, is built of rational reconstructions. A famous quote from a classic book, *Personality in Nature, Society and Culture*, written in 1953 by psychologist Henry Murray and anthropologist Clyde Kluckhohn, sums up some of what we're dealing with here. With the now outdated use of the masculine pronoun as the general form, they summarized their chapter on personality formation with this short and sweet line:

> Every Man is in certain respects, a. like all other men, b. like some other men, c. like no other man.

I want to use "a" and "b" and "c" for a little while to untangle lived experience. The letters alone can get awkward and confusing. So I'll call "a," the human universal part, "universal person" or UP, no directional metaphor implied. The "b" part, the fact that a person also manifests shared group characteristics, I'll call "local person" or LP, no connection to the old "long play" record album. And the "c" part, the unique part that a person claims as uniquely his or her own, I'll call "own person" or OP, no relation to op-ed pieces in the Sunday paper. So UP for the universal part, LP for the local group part, and OP for the unique biographical part.

Don't forget that, in HSR, it's not a question of whether a person is one or another of the three at some particular moment. No one is ever a pure UP, LP or OP. It's a question of the *blend* of all three at any moment. The problem is, most BSS does, in fact, make the unrealistic assumption that a research subject is only one and not the other two.

If a science assumes that subjects are UP, then there won't be any problem generalizing. We're all the same, so whatever is true of anybody is true of everybody else. But if the science only assumes LP, then a group label generalizes everything, stereotyping, in other words, perhaps accurately to some extent. And if research only asumes OP, no one will be like anyone else and generalization will be impossible. In fact, if both researcher and researched consider themselves only OP, it's hard to imagine how they—or any two people for that matter—could ever make sense out of each other's lived experience at all.

We need to consider all three in any rational reconstruction, UP, LP and OP. UP means similarities between any two people are guaranteed by their shared humanity. It makes rational reconstruction of one person by another possible. OP means that differences in point of view will come up, guaranteed, no matter which two people come into contact. There will always be some idiosyncracies. LP means there will be some different patterns that can be generalized among research subjects from a researcher point of view, assuming researcher isn't also an LP as well. OP means differences, LP means some subset of them can be generalized for a group, and UP means there is a shared human basis in terms of which they can be translated.

The hard part of HSR is balancing the UP, the LP and the OP to get a rational reconstruction right. This is the dilemma that Dilthey wanted to figure out. Lived experience means LP and OP.

He doesn't deny UP, nor do I. In fact, in Chapter Six of this book, UP will turn out to be the anchor of common humanity that makes human social science possible at all. But the problem with traditional BSS, Dilthey argues, is that reduction to nerves and muscles makes human social science UP all the way down, UP in a most reductionist sort of way.

The dangerous part of all this is the tendency of humans to assume that we're all UPs, all the time. Social cognition, the descendant of social psychology, calls this the problem of *naive realism*. Naive realism is jargon for the human tendency to think that one's own point of view is objective eternal truth. Any other point of view—any other intentional stance born of lived experience—must be a distortion in need of repair, if not just dumb as a post or a few bulbs short of a chandelier. Naïve realism concludes that differences are an indication that the other person fails as a competent human being. It's very comforting if you can get away with it. *Your* LP and OP are actually *everyone's* UP and therefore nothing to worry about as far as differences go. Any difference is *their* problem, not yours.

Naive realism blocks HSR, but—here is the dangerous part— it does *not* necessarily block BSS. In fact, naive realism can support BSS, because it makes it easier to imagine that "all other things are equal" and that the encounter with human subjects designed and controlled by a researcher is "objective," that is, seen in the same way by everyone. Naïve realism can support a researcher's assumption that an experiment or survey means exactly the same thing to every single subject as it does to the researcher, and to any other researcher who later undertakes the same experiment or survey with any other subjects.

The fact that naive realism is so strong, such a normal part of being human, it makes you think that HSR is a job that humans were designed *not* to do. Remember in the previous chapter how cognitive dissonance set up a problem for John Stuart Mill when he wanted to make induction into a science? It's a similar problem here. Naive realism blocks researching LP and OP points of view. Both cognitive dissonance and naïve realism are parts of being human that encourage us to ignore data that contradict our beliefs, desires, emotions and purposes. Evolution hot-wired us that way. But both these natural human abilities are lethal for human social science.

Mill developed an inductive logic to counter the problem of cognitive dissonance by requiring science to look for negative cases. Now we need another logic, another guideline for thinking, to block naïve realism and guide us into an exploration of other points of view. The logic has to guide us to see different LP and OP intentionalities and help us understand what those differences are so we can rationally reconstruct them. But the same logic has to acknowledge that researcher and researched are also UPs, that it is their shared humanity that makes a translation of their differences possible. That missing logic will be the topic of Chapter Six.

An Example of How BSS Misses a LP

Years ago I was asked to help with an "evaluation" of a tuberculosis outreach program in Baltimore. An article I wrote about the experience is cited in the chapter notes. Senior staff and funders all thought the program was a failure because they hadn't found and treated enough new TB cases. This wasn't naïve realism to them. This was an obvious objective fact born of scientific medicine. They wanted me to dive in and find something worthwhile that the program had accomplished.

I wish I had a nickel for every time a failing program asked for HSR help with an evaluation at the last minute. It was usually a desperate effort to find something good that happened to justify money spent. The strategy always worked, but so did its evil twin, namely, things were also discovered that were worse than expected.

It didn't take long for some good news to appear in my first interviews with outreach workers, the African-American community residents who actually went out and contacted people. When I asked them about the "failure" of the program, they all reacted with descriptions of how, on the contrary, the program had been a "success." The reason was, they had appointed themselves general community resource persons and helped numerous people out in many different ways. It turned out there was a major LP pattern inside the program that had worked well. Outreach worker lived experience was loaded with success.

When I reported this, it amazed the funders and senior staff. It also made them uncomfortable, since it didn't fit into the medical/BSS research design that the foundation required. The good news had been invisible outside their LP identity, but visible inside the LP identity of the outreach workers. Senior staff saw a failure, so that was objective fact and everyone else must feel the same way. This feeling blocked them from making an effort to check with the outreach workers. Why did it require me, an outside HSR type, to hear it and repeat it? Why didn't the outreach workers just tell the senior staff? Why didn't the staff ask?

Any reader who works in an organization of course knows the answer. Issues of hierarchy, and of emotionally loaded habits, get in the way of seeing and saying the obvious, particularly when the obvious isn't visible within the LP point of view of those who control the money and write the rules. In organizational settings, HSR sometimes turns into family therapy, because it makes a group of people aware of their own and others' habitual patterns that are out of awareness. An HSR type can become an organizational developer who can rationally reconstruct people's intentionality and lived experience and then tell them what it is because they can't see it. A guru of business and management, Edgar Schein, actually calls his HSR organizational work "clinical fieldwork."

It's truly amazing, in my experience, how often the boss has a problem that people in her organization have already solved from their OP/ LP points of view which, in turn, is invisible to the boss because it's not part of her lived experience. The old cliché again— If I had a nickel for every time … etc.—only in this case it's true. I really would be rich.

Time on Our Side

Dilthey called his work a "critique of historical reason." Any resemblance to Kant's *Critique of Pure Reason* was purely "intentional"— you should excuse the expression. Dilthey may have been a little scattered, but he was obviously no marketing fool. Then again, the title was a fair enough claim on his part. An emphasis on history cycles throughout his work.

By "history" he means that every human has one, as in lived experience, and that the social and cultural worlds in which those humans live do as well. It means that there is a dance—or maybe a fight—between the two histories as time moves along. History influences biography, and biographies shape history. That little ditty brings us to all the contemporary human social science theories of "structure" and "agency," namely, an understanding that societies and cultures limit what a person can do, but that what a person does changes societies and cultures, and so on back and forth through time in the dialectic that Hegel and later Marx made famous.

Dilthey dives much deeper and travels much more widely with his concept of history than that. He sees individuals as "points of intersection" of different histories, personal and sociocultural, where the intersections shape the lived experience of the moment. For example, any American of my generation has a biography shaped in some way by the Vietnam War, in ways they are aware of and ways in which they are not. Dilthey argues that people don't know themselves historically through pure introspection anyway; instead they see themselves in those parts of history that they objectify. This "objectification" produces artifacts and institutions that then become part of reality. Like the Vietnam Memorial Wall in Washington and "Rolling Thunder" when thousands of vets from all over the country ride their motorcycles to D.C. on Memorial Day.

Dilthey works the history concept in many ways that are beyond the scope of this book. For now, it is enough to see that lived experience and intentionality take their shape and change along a continuum of time, sometimes in surprising ways, the past and the future always a part of the configuration of the present. His concept echoes a human version of the weather in Lorenz's computer model and how it changed so dramatically. Understanding is something that happens over time.

We've returned to nonlinear dynamic country, to the concept of path dependence, only now with human intentionality and lived experience folded into it. Lived experience is a path, to some extent unpredictable, possibly taking dramatic and surprising turns. As the old joke goes, "You want to make god laugh? Tell him *your* plans."

You see how Dilthey really did mount his horse, call it "History," and ride off in all directions? But the general point he was making stands out—There is a horse and you do need to ride it. Lived experience, and the intentionality it interacts with, are *dynamic*. They move together through time, for subjects and researchers both. Hegel, the original anti-Newton and founder of the historical tradition in which Dilthey trained, produced a famous and elegant quote: "The owl of Minerva spreads its wings only with the falling of the dusk." Or, to rephrase another variation on the theme in Joni Mitchell's more direct terms, "You don't know what you've got 'til it's gone."

History is missing in most human social science, of all types, a casualty of efforts to imitate the timelessness of natural science and its laws and its laboratory. Marx is the obvious counterexample, though his history was mechanical rather than nonlinear. There are famous longitudinal BSS studies, though not many because they are expensive, and certainly there are historical studies based on archives and artifacts. My take on it, though, is that history—the dynamics, the dimension of time, the path dependencies—still tends to be neglected.

Except for the second law of thermodynamics, the natural science tradition is by and large without time. Cycles and oscillations maybe, but not contingent paths with unexpected futures. That timeless view is what BSS carried forward from the Enlightenment. And so did the HSR that I trained in, anthropology and linguistics. We researched how things worked at a particular point in time. This is how this place *is*. This is how these people *are*. This is what a certain kind of person *is* like. This *is* how everyone talks. Linguistics even has a name for the approach— "synchronic"—meaning "without time."

Remember my Subaru Forester? Everything I described in the previous chapter was about how it works in some timeless way. If Dilthey ran a garage, he would adjust his gimme cap with "Metaphysics Sucks" embroidered on it and shake his head when I asked for an isolated timeless cause. "History," he would say, "history is where understanding and explanation lie, my boy. You want to know why you have to buy new tires so soon? Because recent market pressure means they put cheaper tires on new cars to save money. Your gas gauge suddenly shows empty? A mouse probably ate the cable. Why do you have mice in your garage? If you're going to keep the car rather than buy a new one, then we really oughtta change the water pump when we replace the timing belt, because it'll cost a fortune to get to it later. You know those cloth grocery bags, hiking poles, and sheetrock scraps in the back? You're kind of a green type, aren't you? Except shouldn't you be using adobe instead of sheetrock for your walls? You live in New Mexico, for god's sake. Not very culturally authentic of you.

The concept of lived experience means that HSR *has to* have history in it, in all the ways Dilthey described. Whatever kind of science HSR is to be, it will have to be dynamic. It will have to show how human social life works over time. It will have to be *diachronic*, "through time," as the linguists say. It will use the past, recent and distant, to understand and explain the present and glimpse the near future. And it will have to learn and weave together different first person points of view, a major task that will occupy most of Chapter Six.

Is Reality a Dream?

Dilthey takes intentionality and sets it on the ground of human social reality and puts it in motion. Before I leave him for the next chapter, I'd like to show how he handled one concept that makes people who contemplate HSR nervous, and rightly so, the notion of *Reality* with a capital "real." We give the researcher the duty of being part of the science. Are there any limits to the lies he can tell? Rational reconstructions. Points of view. All well and good. But, once it's done, does it tell us anything about the "real" world?

BSS, under the flag of natural science, doesn't worry much about reality. Of course science describes objective reality. That's what science does by definition. But for HSR, reality is more of a headache, not to mention heartache. HSR brings into a project different human subjects, different lived experiences, different intentionalities, and different points of view. Even after naive realism is sedated, HSR still has to deal with different notions of "what is real." And just to spice up the recipe, those different views will overlap, sometimes a lot, sometimes a little. Recall the UP, LP and OP of the earlier sections in this chapter? Each of us is a human like all, like some, and like no other? For any two of us, our descriptions of a particular reality will be similar, but also different because of social category, and for sure idiosyncratic, all at once. How do we make this mess into a science?

I'm not going to get lost in an argument about whether or not our lives are actually extraterrestrial dreams. We did that under the influence of different substances when I was in college. The fantasy never seems to stop though. I just received an email saying that the Mayan prophecy for the end of the world in late 2012 was accurate and we're now in the afterlife.

The problem of different realities when humans research other humans pushes difficult questions into the conversation that HSR has to deal with, questions that BSS should deal with but usually ignores. The first annoying question is, who controls what goes into the conclusion of a research report? What part of the conclusion is *real*? In the end, whose intentionality, based on what kind of lived experience, decides what shapes a researcher's book or film or museum exhibit that claims to describe and explain research subjects?

This is an old problem. Who gets to say what happened? The rulers or the people? The winners or the losers of history? The managers or the employees? The funders or the researchers? The board or the stockholders? The consultant or the clients? And, of course, the researchers or the subjects?

There's a famous movie a reader could watch, recommended for all who are interested in human social science. It is called *Rashomon*, an old Kurosawa film from 1950. Different people give an account of a murder and rape. The point of the movie is how much the stories differ from each other. The title of the film became human social science jargon, "The Rashomon Effect." A colleague of mine wrote an article about it, cited in the chapter notes. HSR accepts the Rashomon Effect as normal. But then how do we, the researchers, reconcile our own view with the different views of subjects when we present a conclusion? How do we make a science out of that? The scientist just takes over in the end? The subjects write their own book? They take turns, page by page? What?

In the *real* world, it's never purely one voice that completely dominates. Even in extreme cases of control and oppression, humans can still *resist*. Ever ordered your kid to do something and they do it, sort of, in some minimal literal way, but not really, and then look at you and scratch their nose with their middle finger? That's resistance.

Still, one particular type of subject, in the end, does dominate when scientific reality is declared. In BSS research, the dominant voice is that of the researcher, period. The rules of the traditional scientific method require it. HSR, unlike BSS, accepts that interaction among several different lived experiences and intentionalities is the empirical bedrock of their science. "Objective" is not a possible description of how HSR works. It is not researcher and "object" of research, because the "object" is also a "subject." HSR produces something that emerges out of that interaction, some kind of joint creation of scientist and subjects that allows a researcher to talk about subjects in a way that includes rather than pretends to control their intentionality and lived experience.

As a preview of what is to come later in the book, think of human social science as *intersubjective.* The choice between *objective* or *subjective* just doesn't make sense. It doesn't solve any "reality" problems because the distinction is "unreal" to start with. HSR is something that happens "between subjects," one or more of whom happens to be a researcher and one or more of whom happen to be those who are researched. When human social science claims to be "objective," it misses the point of how the science works. If it claims to be "subjective," on the other hand, it misses the point of being a science.

I'll explore what a "scientific intersubjectivity" might look like starting in the next chapter using a different kind of logic, and, in the chapter after that, with a way to handle researcher/subject encounters using a concept of translation, and in the chapter after that, by looking at how human interests shape a project. But for now I'll just leave it at how HSR, on the ground, works the space between researchers and subjects in an evidence-based, logical, falsifiable way. "Scientific intersubjectivity," unlike "objective human social science," is *not* an oxymoron.

Reality is Kicking a Rock

A second difficult question about reality that Dilthey dredges up: The problem philosophers have is, how does the knowledge that a human subject constructs—whether researcher or researched—correspond to reality with a capital R, reality as something that exists out there independent of any humans who might stumble across and try to make sense of it?

Intentionality interacts with lived experience and fuses into a point of view in some context, all well and good. But is it the UP option in the earlier quote, we're all alike and our reality is just a "mirror of nature," to borrow the title of Richard Rorty's famous book? Any mind will have the same view if you dunk it in the same reality? Or is it the OP option, reality is a completely personal idiosyncratic view that has nothing to do with what anyone else says is really out there, assuming that something is? They call that *solipsism*—the only thing you can be sure of is that your own mind exists. Or maybe it's an LP option, particularly important when someone works in worlds where researcher and subjects are members of the same social category. What you see is socially constructed and held in place by power.

None of the above can win the argument on their own, and none of the three 19th century philosophers discussed in this book—Mill, Brentano and Dilthey—argued any of those extremes. Lived experience is a mix of point of view and real world. But what kind of a mix? How to describe it? As the philosophers would put it, what exists—ontology—and how do we come to know it—epistemology? And if a reader is among those who think brain science is taking care of the problem, just mention "qualia" and listen to the expert tell you, while the fMRI hums in the background, that qualia is the great unanswered question of their field. Qualia, a reader has probably already guessed if she didn't know it already, means "subjective conscious experience."

Human social science, of whatever type, has to get clear on what claims it is making about reality with a capital R. I'm remembering when one of my graduate advisers told me about the moment he decided to sign my dissertation. It eventually

turned into a book called *Ripping and Running* about the world
of heroin addicts, and part of it described how the heroin was
prepared and injected and what effects it could have. Right after
he read it, he told me, he went to see a movie—it might have
been *Panic in Needle Park*. The movie had scenes with an addict
who was about to inject. My adviser said, with respect in his
voice, "I knew what was going to happen." Whatever reality is,
the movie and I described something out there in the same way.
No surprise, really, because there were "real" limits on what had
to happen. Powder had to be dissolved in water and injected into
a vein. Endorphins then flooded neural circuits. Physics and
biology made for some universals in the HSR.

Dilthey deals with this question of "reality" at the level of the
human social world in a way I like. A title of another of his books
sums it up: *The Origin of Our Belief in the Reality of the External
World and Its Justification* (1890). How do humans know what
is real? The key is, reality is first felt as a *resistance to one's will.
Reality starts when the purpose part of intentionality doesn't work.* A
colleague from sociology put it very well. One day he told me that
people accused him of always getting what he wanted. He told
them, no, when he sees he's not going to get something, he stops
wanting it. A mix of Dilthey and Buddha.

Reality emerges from action in the world, based on how the
world makes it easy or difficult for us to live our everyday lives.
Dilthey's view of reality as resistance to will takes us towards an
ecological/evolutionary way of thinking, lived experience not just
as a situation, but as something that happens dynamically in an
"environment," that is a lively and active partner. For now I'll just
say that reality is grounded in action/reaction/action cycles for a
subject in the context of his own lived experience based on his
own intentional stance. Reality is about *limits* that the world sets

on the action we can take. We either have to *adapt* to those limits or *change* them, but we can't ignore them if we want to realize our intentions.

If those limits, that resistance to human will, hold up for *any* human doing *anything anywhere* at *any time*, we've found reality in a human universal sense of the term. In one famous story, Samuel Johnson made the same point. He was reacting against the subjective arguments of Berkeley's philosophy. The world, Johnson wanted to show, was more than just sense impressions in a human mind. "I refute it thus," he supposedly said. While he said it, he kicked a rock. I can't find any sources that report what he muttered when he grabbed his foot in pain. But he made his point; reality was a rock when you kicked it. Resistance, guaranteed, every time by anyone anywhere, unless it was a foam Hollywood rock or an artificial limb, but in that case neither the rock nor the limb would be "real." Unless you were a film production designer in the former case, or a returning vet from Iraq in the latter, in which case they would be very "real" in a different way.

Remember the story of my great-grandfather emigrating from Ireland? The main reason he left was the potato famine. Anyone, anywhere, who experiences a famine will feel that famine *resist* what it is possible for them to do, not to mention threaten to end their ability to do anything. Lack of food is a reality whose "resistance" to the will of human subjects is the same everywhere, whoever the subject is, whenever they live. "World hunger" is a *real* problem, a Universal Person fact.

In Chapter Six, I'll use this particular version of reality under the name of "human universals." Resistance to will brings in the "real world" objects of the natural sciences and the "real world" human environment of resources and power, but it brings them in as they *effect human subject lived experiences*, because that is the phenomenon that HSR focuses on. Human subjects and reality are both in the research, and the human subjects, well, they're not a mirror of nature. They're more like the distorting mirrors in a carnival, except "distort" is a negative word and the kind of mirror I'm thinking of isn't. Maybe *intentional mirror* might be the right words to use.

If you want to know the length of time a certain amount of heat requires to dissolve heroin powder in water, you do physics and chemistry. If you want to know what it's like to be a junkie cooking up when the sickness of withdrawal is rumbling inside you, what they called "the snake" in Baltimore, you do HSR.

Dilthey's Long Ride.

It was quite a ride, the one Dilthey took on that horse that went in all directions, even if he never did arrive at a final destination. He was disappointed that he didn't finish the job. As his translator said:

> The fascination with human life in toto, the conviction that "man" is to be found not in some abstract philosophical definition but amid a historical-cultural process that continuously "defines' him and then partially "undefines" him by way of a continually expanding process of "redefinition" meant in effect that whatever success Dilthey might achieve in his enterprise must be provisional, partial, and permanently corrigible (pg. 9).

Perhaps Dilthey tried to solve too many related problems instead of just the one big problem—how to create a *Geisteswissenschaft*, a way of learning and conveying knowledge *about* some people *by* other people that would yield more profound and more accurate results than anything the Naturwissenschaft model could deliver. But even if he didn't pull it all together as he rode his horse every which way, he visited some interesting places. He may not have arrived at a final destination, but it was one hell of a ride. If Jack Kerouac hadn't already used the title, his collected works could be renamed *On The Road*.

Towards the end, in the final stages of his long career, he closed in on the idea of *interpretation* as a key to what HSR was all about. Most readers probably aren't familiar with the term "hermeneutics." It's from a classical Greek word meaning "translate" or "interpret." It advises that you have to know the whole to understand the parts and the parts to understand the whole. In that way it, too, echoes the earlier discussion in this book of nonlinear dynamics. That catchy principle is called the "hermeneutic circle," which would be a good name for a jazz quartet. I haven't developed that part of Dilthey here, but we will head his way with the concept of translation in the chapter after next.

HSR gets easier to understand once you realize that "science" doesn't mean just one thing. That is a core and lasting conclusion that Dilthey established. Contemplating an alternative human social science isn't as hard as it used to be. It's our job, in an era when HSR is of more widespread public interest than it ever has been before, to continue the work by standing on the shoulders of the giants, three of whom—Dilthey, Brentano, and Mill—I've used selectively in this book. These aren't the only three I could have picked, not by a long shot. We could go back to the Greeks or forward to the growing number of researchers in the HSR profession today. But those three were among the first in the modern Western incarnation of human social science. Having returned to a sample of their work in preparation for this book, I can see the power of what they did in defining the space I work in today. It isn't always easy to reach back across the centuries, but I hope the reader found it useful and is inspired to take a closer look at the ancestors for him or herself. They all thought deeply about how to understand who we are and why we act the way we do. They merit a fresh reading as human social science remodels itself for a new era.

What is Human Social Research About?

That is the question that I wanted the three 19th century founders to answer. After more than fifteen years working in the world where people have asked me to do HSR, nervous at times about the sanity of their request but driven by frustration at lack of useful BSS results, I wanted to go back to the founders to get help in better articulating what HSR does and why it is a science in the fundamental sense of that word.

    The founders taught me that the basic issues have been around for a couple of centuries. Humans in their social worlds represent a different kind of phenomenon for a science, and that phenomenon has characteristics that the founders of natural science didn't take into account, logically enough, because *their* phenomenon didn't have those characteristics. At the heart of it, human social worlds have to be described to a great extent in terms of subject intentionality as it shapes and is modified by lived experience over time.

    "Subjective" versus "objective" no longer makes much sense, since everyone involved is a subject. Like any science, HSR requires evidence, logic and falsification, no question about that. But at base it is a science built from encounters among subjects, including researchers who, like it or not, are also subjects. HSR is *intersubjective*. Asking whether it is objective or subjective is like measuring computer capacity in cubic feet. It doesn't answer the question, which is, am I willing to make a decision based on the results of this research? Can I believe this information? On what grounds?

What counts as evidence, logic and falsification for HSR isn't going to look like traditional models of hypothesis testing. Evidence will come from many sources and be built up into rational reconstructions. Mill's inductive logic, with its emphasis on negative cases, will live on, but it needs an engine in it to make it a more dynamic, and we need additional logics that can adapt to how learning occurs and changes the research path even as the research is done. Falsification will be ongoing rather than a philosophy or a single test, and it will have to falsify interacting patterns rather than just a static hypothesis built out of a few causal variables.

HSR truly is a different kind of science. Several modern concepts that weren't available to it back in the 19th century help put it on a firmer foundation now. But then how is this different science supposed to work? To explore that question, I want to shift from the Germans to a Brit to help with an answer, though he studied with an Austrian and then immigrated to Chicago and wound up in Southern California, a post-structural life if ever there was one. He came up with a model for *making a case*. His model could include evidence from the traditional laboratory, or not, but it also opened up many other possibilities for evidence, logic and falsification. It showed how multiple points of view could be put together into a single scientific argument. That's where we're headed in the next chapter.

CHAPTER FOUR

Taking HSR to Court

Brentano—Dilthey even more so—wanted a way to talk "science" and "human social reality" at the same time. Western Enlightenment science just wasn't their cup of hemlock. I don't mean to consign BSS to the dustbin of history here, as if anyone should, or could even if they wanted to. But really, thinking about what BSS has produced—in terms of its aspirations to be the definitive experimental science of humans—what have we learned after a couple of hundred years about how the human social world works? It's probably no accident that the BSS discussion of "ecological validity" is comparatively recent and somewhat neglected. Recall that the concept is the way BSS asks itself what relevance their research results have to the real world. Ecological validity is the crazy old relative locked in the attic that you don't want your dinner guests to meet.

But then HSR hasn't exactly been a lighthouse on the shoals either. Its lack of clarity and use of convoluted jargon are legendary. Worse, a fair number of contemporary HSR royalty reject the word "science" completely, as deluded in their own way as the BSS claim that the experimental laboratory is the only possible thing that "science" can mean. Brentano and Dilthey, the 19th century heroes of this book, unloaded concepts that have kept HSR busy in academic industries of fog production right up until the present day. The pieces of an alternative human social science have been around for a long time, one of the reasons why I chose examples from the 19ᵗʰ century. A clear and coherent overview of an HSR science has not.

In the next three chapters I want to try to develop such a coherent view based on the 19ᵗʰ century foundations. I'm just one in a long list of people who have made the effort, but I come at it from a different angle and hope that might add something to the previous attempts of many other colleagues. The angle is, I want to describe, in a clear and coherent way, what HSR can do and how it can do it for the growing number of non-researchers engaged with the human social world who want better ways of understanding how it works. I've been at this kind of thing since I left the university in the mid-1990s, and for quite a while before that. The people I've worked with over the years are the ones who have done the most to help me write this book, and for that I thank them and hope it earns their interest and proves to be of use.

Given that purpose, the next step in building an overview of HSR, it seems to me, is to return to the basic idea already mentioned in the introduction, that any science requires evidence organized according to some logic with systematic attempts to falsify its conclusions. That notion, taken together with the attitude of "abandon the laboratory all ye who enter here," means that HSR needs a different way to think about the science trinity—evidence, logic and falsification. I'll start this chapter with another philosopher that I've used in talks about this problem for years, often amazed that many in human social science audiences had never heard of him. An alternative to the laboratory is exactly what he had in mind.

The Anglo-German Hybrid

Stephen Toulmin just passed away, in December of 2009, and that was a shame, for all the normal reasons, but also because he was, as far as I know, one of the few who offered a clear alternative to the experimental tradition for human social science. I admired him for other reasons as well. I aspire to his "law of composition," that the "effort the writer does not put into writing, the reader has to put into reading." And I like his humor. The law of composition, he pointed out, was particularly important to enforce with philosophers, where "obscurity is regarded as a mark of profundity."

Toulmin was a Londoner by birth. He took classes with Ludwig Wittgenstein, the Austrian genius who revolutionized philosophy not once, but twice. Wittgenstein, too, is worth a long digression that I will not attempt here. His genius is reflected in his preference for mysteries and movies over academic tomes that expound abstract truths free of the context that inevitably messes them up. From Wittgenstein, Toulmin inherited skepticism towards any and all universal proclamations, a view of reason as grounded and practical, and a career dedicated to showing that human reasoning was a mix of what was true anywhere and what was only true under the particular circumstances of a specific case.

Toulmin has always surprised me because he pops up at unexpected times. Not so long ago, I was summoned to a panel of the National Research Council. This is supposed to be an honor, and it is in a way, but I'd already been disillusioned with our national center of science when they micromanaged committee reports to make them conform to "war on drugs" ideology in the late 1970s. I was on that panel, too.

This more recent invitation landed in my email a few years

after President George W. Bush had proclaimed his education policy, called "No Child Left Behind." The political agenda behind the summons was to question the idea of basing educational policy primarily on standardized tests. BSS dreams of *standardization*. All other things have to be equal except what's being measured, as John Stuart Mill said long ago, and the measurement has to work exactly the same way in every case. The problem is that the range of schools, students, teachers and communities included in a national policy are anything but standardized, or, to stretch the grammar, standardizable. The panel needed a talking head to say that and, at the time, I worked at the University of Maryland, only a Metro ride away, so I was a cheap date.

Educational research is heavily BSS, like most human social science, and those kinds of researchers were the majority on the panel and in the audience. But education is one of those areas that has supported HSR, so a couple of us HSR types were invited as well.

It's an interesting historical footnote: By and large, HSR development in the latter part of the 20th century occurred in disciplines oriented to practice. Therefore, due to the long-standing pathology of separating theory and practice in the U.S., they ranked lower in the academic pecking order. They had nothing to lose and everything to gain by trying something new, especially when what they actually did never made it into the BSS literature that claimed to describe them. I'll never forget my mother and her teacher friends laughing over the latest nonsense with which the academic in-service training expert had just wasted half their day. HSR, with its focus on lived experience in their actual world, bubbled up for its political value. Ray Rist wrote an article in a1980 education journal called "Blitzkrieg Ethnography: On the Transformation of a Method into a Movement."

The problem for the organizers of the panel at the National Research Council was, what kind of circus tent could they raise to make those different academic acts fit into the same show? Toulmin was the answer the staff came up with. I was pleasantly surprised, astounded even. It was the main reason I accepted the invitation. I'd been a fan for years but had seldom heard his name uttered in polite company. He had written for educators as well as philosophers and was known in that world. His teacher, Wittgenstein, had actually taught in elementary schools in the Austrian mountains between World Wars. Something about their connection with teaching kept both of them aware of real situations, how they worked, and what sorts of concepts were most useful in figuring them out.

The Courtroom Model

Toulmin wrote a book called *The Uses of Argument* in 1958. It is his most famous work, because it lays out a *theory of argumentation* that percolated into all kinds of places, although not into mainstream science. True to the spirit of practical reason, the book found its way into educational curricula at many different levels. It also inspired a field of linguistics that spawned numerous books and articles. But, right now, I want to use his theory like the National Research Council panel did, as a framework for a HSR that can include, but not be limited by, the laboratory tradition of the natural sciences.

The diagram of Toulmin's theory—let's call it a "model"—comes with slight variations. Here's one straightforward version among dozens that you can find on the Internet:

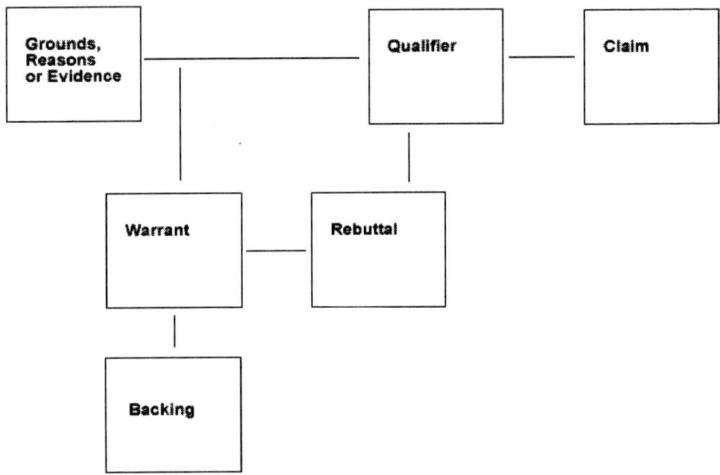

Toulmin calls this a model for an argument. I think of it as *making a case*. The diagram shows the elements needed to make a case and how those elements are interrelated. With this diagram, he shifted the metaphor for human social science from the *laboratory* to the *courtroom*.

Let's walk through the picture. The big three in the diagram are the *grounds* and the *claim* and the *warrant*. Making a claim is the ultimate purpose of it all, as shown in the box on the far right of the diagram. Everything else is organized around getting to that box. It is the "therefore" or "in conclusion" part of making a case, the part where you cue the trumpets and take a bow.

The grounds, also called "reasons" or "evidence" in the diagram, are the materials gathered and organized to support the claim. "Reasons" and "evidence" don't mean the same thing, but let that go by for now. I'll just use the term "grounds" here. And why should anyone believe that those grounds lead to that conclusion? Because the *warrant* says they do. And if you don't believe the warrant, there is another box right below it that justifies the warrant called the *backing*.

The *qualifier* has to do with the strength of the claim. Are you certain about the claim, or just pretty sure, or maybe you think it's at least a possibility, or you've been to law school and you're presenting a worst case scenario that will probably never happen? And finally, the last of the boxes in the diagram is the *rebuttal*. You consider the counterarguments to the case you are making even as you make it, usually to acknowledge and answer them before someone raises them.

All the science elements that we need are in the diagram. Evidence organized by a logic with qualification and falsification built in. It's easy to see how BSS fits this diagram, at least in its simple form. The claim is a hypothesis deduced from a theory. The grounds are a structured and bounded set of data in numerical form—usually an experiment or a survey. The warrants are the usual research design and statistical analysis by a software package that manipulates the numbers with a cutoff value where you accept or reject the claim. The backing? A couple of centuries of traditional science, exactly what I'm excavating in this book. The qualification? If the BSS is any good there will be several, often summarized at the end of an article with a line about how more research needs to be done. The rebuttal was already included in a null hypothesis that there is "no relationship" between the variables. And there you have it. As Tony Soprano used to say, badabing, badaboom, BSS in a Toulmin format.

Does the diagram work for HSR? It works pretty well there, too, except the way it's going to work in practice is more complicated than BSS, just like lived experience is more complicated than the "data" produced by a tightly-wrapped BSS research design. That difference is what the rest of this chapter will be about.

The conclusion for the moment is that Toulmin's "making a case" model broadens the concept of science well beyond what can be accomplished in a laboratory using the experimental method. It makes a case based on evidence and logic that support a conclusion. It sets up a claim so that it can be challenged. And remember that the diagram is based on a courtroom model, so there will also be cross-examination by opponents and evaluation by a judge and possibly a jury, what academics usually lump together under the phrase "peer review."

Toulmin's work has another advantage, not the primary reason to consider it, but useful all the same. Most readers of *The Lively Science* won't be professional human social scientists. For those readers, from the outside looking in, a *courtroom* rather than a *laboratory* gives a better intuitive feel for how HSR works right from the beginning. A courtroom is familiar to most people, usually not for the most pleasant of reasons. And the popularity of TV shows like the famous Judge Judy helps as well. As Chris Rock used to say in a TV ad, "Before you go to court, watch court TV." The courtroom conjures up images of making a case using many different kinds of grounds from the lived experience and intentionalities of human actors in a social world. That's exactly what HSR aspires to.

Besides, the diagram applies to more than HSR and BSS. Toulmin later used it to organize his research with physicians, with particular attention to the time pressure of emergencies and the moral weight of life and death decisions. I know from my own experience that it can also serve as a model for journalism, law enforcement and intelligence analysis, not to mention history, not to mention fixing a house or a car. In fact, in his later work, Toulmin generalizes his ideas into a framework for "practical reason," whatever it is one might be doing in whatever kind of situation one is doing it.

HSR can be understood as an example of Toulmin's diagram.

BSS can as well. HSR will have to use Toulmin in a different way, a way that breaks many BSS rules. The diagram has to guide a different kind of learning, a different kind of research practice, and a different kind of claim about what its conclusions represent. But it will still be evidence organized by a logic that is capable of challenge by colleagues, research subjects and audiences.

Human Social Science: Land of Contrasts

Toulmin lives up to his "composition rule," mentioned at the start of this chapter. He works hard to make it easy on a reader. His diagram is one of the clearest sources used in this book. And it is helpful, because it spotlights some of the major differences between two approaches to human social science. In order to continue building HSR, I want to use Toulmin to cast some of those differences in sharp relief.

The first major difference is this: The diagram is a template for a goal that HSR needs to reach, *not* a recipe for how to get there. It tells you what you need to have at the end. With BSS, on the other hand, Toulmin's diagram can serve as a step-by-step guide for traditional research design. Its application will be pretty linear. It will be similar to a musician putting the score on the music stand and playing it. Or to an actor taking a screenplay, sitting in a chair at audition, and reading it. The relationship between score or script and what actually happens is close. It's easy to see the one in the other.

There is, of course, room for innovation in BSS research. A BSS scientist might well spend a lot of time preparing some particular part of the diagram—coming up with an "instrument," as they call it in survey research, or a clever experimental "manipulation." (It's always bothered me that human social science thinks of itself as based on "instruments" and "manipulations.") But once the pieces are in place, like they are in a musical score or a screenplay, BSS is pretty boilerplate. Do this, then do this, etc. Imagination can return at the end with the number-tweaking and interpreting.

It's supposed to work that way. Remember, BSS carries forward from the natural sciences the idea that making a case is a scientist-controlled process that any other scientist should be able to *replicate* anywhere else in exactly the same way. A scientist sets up the plan—writes the score or the screenplay—and then follows it carefully. And then she can hand the plan over to anyone else, and that person can play the music or read the lines in pretty much the same way.

With HSR, Toulmin's model is more a guide to improvisation. The diagram shows a HSR researcher where she needs to end up, but it is *not* a score or a screenplay to follow step-by-step as the work is actually done. Even more interesting, what the boxes in the diagram require will change as the research goes along and the scientist learns more about what needs to be in them.

Think about something you recently learned how to do out there in the human social world. It could be something trivial, like finding out about a new store and going there to make a purchase. Or it could be more complicated than that, like moving to or even just exploring a new neighborhood. Or it could be life altering, like having a kid or starting—or losing—a job. Or it could be culture-shocking, like a move from a middle-class American life to work for an NGO in an impoverished war-torn country where you don't know the language. In all these cases, from the trivial to the profound, you have to start to figure out the new world after you get there and keep figuring it out as you go. You make mistakes and rethink what you thought you'd figured out already.

This kind of learning, one or another version of which any

reader will have experienced, is a cousin to HSR, although you were just learning new surroundings or maybe looking for a little adventure. The thought of producing a credible scientific report of your experience was the furthest thing from your mind. Still, the examples contain an essential HSR ingredient—you *adapt* your own intentionality to a different lived experience in order to figure something out. I'll bet that whichever example you were thinking of had as part of the story the unscheduled and improvised and opportunistic ways you learned, not to mention how you drew on different kinds of information, some of it that fell into your lap, some of it that you went looking for, some of it that you intuited.

HSR takes something humans normally do—learn a new human social world—and makes it more transparent and systematic so that it becomes a science. In contrast to BSS, though, "systematic" doesn't mean a pre-defined step-by-step process. Instead, HSR works by keeping an eye on Toulmin's model, the goal of making a claim, while moving around among the boxes. A researcher repeatedly asks himself, "This is where I need to get to. How much of what I need to get there do I have? What do I do next to get more?" HSR is more like steering towards a goal through unknown terrain where the goal only becomes clear after you drive for a while. The metaphor for BSS would be more like following directions block by block with a GPS on the dashboard. If an HSR researcher used this metaphorical GPS, it would always be talking in that annoying digital voice about how you didn't follow directions on that last turn and the GPS now has to recalculate.

For HSR, research in real time will be fluid and dynamic and open to new content and surprising changes in direction. What a researcher does at time T will depend on what was learned at time T - 1. Nothing new here. It's the same path dependence described earlier. HSR has to be path-dependent, because a researcher learns more about the lived experience and intentionality of subjects *after* the research is underway, and the longer it is underway, the more he knows about what he needs to learn next.

If you are a BSS type, HSR looks like you handed the musical score over to Charley Parker and he played it and you wondered what in the world that he thought he was doing. As the story goes, musician Cab Calloway sneered that it was "Chinese music," a slur meaning that to him it made no musical sense. Similarly with a screenplay, it's like you compare the final film with the original screenplay and wonder what happened, particularly if you're the author of the novel on which the screenplay was based. HSR in real time is more like the *improvisation* of jazz and the *collaboration* of filmmaking than it is like a controlled sequence of pre-defined steps.

But, in the end, any human social scientist still has to *make a case*. That's where HSR and BSS come together as science—at the end, not during the work itself. A story, said Aristotle in one of those quotes that make you wonder how he managed to dominate Western thought for all those centuries, has a beginning, a middle, and an end. HSR and BSS meet at the end, but they differ at the beginning and in the middle. That's a lot of difference.

Toulmin's "making a case" model allows this difference. The experimental method does not.

HSR and Qualitative

Here's a second difference that Toulmin's diagram helps us see. Most people associate HSR only with *qualitative* research, and BSS with *quantitative*. It ain't necessarily so, speaking of Cab Calloway. "Qualitative" is at base only about the data and nothing else. Qualitative data are propositions; quantitative data are numbers.

The HSR outlined in this book uses quantitative data all the time. In fact, I've never written an ethnography without numbers in it. I use them differently, but then that's the point, data of all kinds are used in HSR, and Toulmin's diagram can handle that as well.

Years ago I did a brief study based on an aggregate data set with Owen Murdoch. We called it "quanltative" research—pronounced like "kwaneltative"—just to mess with peoples' minds. The question the research sponsors asked was, how come these epidemiological statistics are moving around in a peculiar way? We went out and talked to a sample of people who *were* the numbers and a sample of people who *reported* the numbers and found out. HSR by the numbers, so to speak. In a similar kind of project a few years later, I edited a special issue of a journal with Nick Kozel and entitled it "Talking Numbers."

HSR isn't about the *kind* of data you use, propositional versus numeric—or visual or tactile or olfactory or any other kind. It's about how to *learn* about a human social world. That's why I don't want this book to be read as a "qualitative" research book. It is a *human social science book* built on the 19th century assumption that a Geisteswissenschaft—Dilthey's awkward sounding word—is a different kind of science from Naturwissenschaft. The raw material out of which the "Wissenschaft" is built—whether it is propositions or numbers or both plus other things—isn't the point at all. The point is the different epistemology in play, not the kind of data it plays with.

The heart of the difference is this: With BSS, the centerpiece of Toulmin's diagram is a hypothesis that a researcher creates to be *tested* in a pre-planned tightly structured way. With HSR, a researcher doesn't start with a hypothesis. A research question, but not a hypothesis in the traditional sense of the term. Instead, a hypothesis is *discovered* and *constructed as part of the research*, using whatever it takes to get what a researcher needs to fill in the boxes in Toulmin's diagram to justify and then potentially falsify it.

Intersubjectivity

Here's a third difference between HSR and BSS that Toulmin's framework handles better than an experimental lab. As mentioned earlier, HSR rejects the choice between "subjective" and "objective." The concepts miss the point of how to evaluate the research. In any human social science, *everyone* is a subject, a thinking, feeling conscious (sometimes) being, that fact being at the heart of the arguments by Brentano and Dilthey as to why it is a different kind of science. On the other hand, it *is* a science, not just the personal hallucination of a researcher, also something that Brentano and Dilthey argued.

HSR is *intersubjective*, a science that is done *between subjects*. Toulmin's diagram can easily represent BSS with its delusions of objectivity. But—another great advantage it has over the model of an experiment—it can handle HSR intersubjectivity as well.

How can it do this? Notice that Toulmin's model organizes what a researcher learns. As the HSR diagram gets filled in, it's part a researcher construction and part research subject words and actions. It's a structure to make sense of research subjects' first person points of view from a researcher-outsider's point of view, but the insider subjects provide most of the material used to build it. *Everyone* is in the science. *Including* the researcher. In the end, it's hard to pull the pieces apart.

Can you smell the smoke? This is the scene in the old sci-fi movies where the human gives the Hollywood version of a computer a paradoxical order and the machine whirrs and shakes and lights flash and smoke comes out of it and it fizzles out in a shower of sparks. Examples of such paradoxes that many readers will know include Russell's paradox and Gödel's incompleteness theorem. Even more well known are examples like the sentence "This sentence is false," which was actually one of the commands Capt. Kirk used to blow up a computer in an ancient *Star Trek* episode, or the Magritte painting of a pipe called "This is not a pipe." These all introduce the horror of *self-reference*, "horror" because when something refers to itself all sorts of peculiar un-orderly things can happen. "Intersubjective" implies "self-reference," no way around it, because the researcher becomes part of the research, and, more confounding yet, the research itself is an example of a human social world that happens when a human social world is being researched.

Personally I think self-reference provides good comedy material, like the career politician who says we need to elect him to get all those political insiders out of office, or the expert who tells an audience that they shouldn't believe the experts. Once I was working on an academic article with three colleagues from the English Department who were worried about a complicated point we were making. I suggested we just add a footnote, "For more information see this article." I think it was at that point that they made me fourth author on the title page.

It's always struck me as a funny story, how two interesting self-reference problems both happened in the 1920s. On the one hand, Werner Heisenberg invented the uncertainty principle for physics, and physics picked it up and ran with it. The scientist was part of the experiment, no big deal. On the other hand, HSR researchers working in a Westinghouse factory discovered that the main reason workers improved their performance was because they enjoyed being paid attention to by the researchers. This became known as the "Hawthorne effect," named after the part of the factory where the work was done. Human social science, rather than accepting that the scientist was part of the science like the physicists did, decided that this was an "effect" to be eliminated at all costs. Finally, eighty-some years later, we might be catching up to reality. Of course the scientist is part of the science. It is intersubjective.

Human social science is a collaboration between scientists and subjects. All of them contribute to how it is done and what it concludes. Toulmin's diagram can handle this, because a researcher can fill it with material that subjects provide to make a case about the cases they make. As they say in Austrian German, BSS "can't even begin with this." Science, any science, is supposed to strive for "objectivity," meaning no researcher effects, no self-reference, no attention to the lived experience of how the science was done.

Every time I talk about this key characteristic of HSR—*both* researcher *and* subject intentionality and lived experience as part of the science—I think of my favorite BSS to HSR conversion story. Years ago an unassuming guy came up to chat with me at a linguistics meeting. It turned out he was, still is, a well-known social psychologist who worked at Massachusetts General Hospital. "It was the damnedest thing," he more or less said—I'm reporting from memory and making his words up; he was much more articulate. He'd walk with a patient to an interview room and chat, then sit in the room and ask the standard BSS questions to measure the patient on some psychological scale, then walk with the patient back out to the front door, chatting away. The thing that drove him crazy was that the chats taught him more about the patient than the scale did.

His name is Eliot Mishler, and he was exploring ways to make those interesting chats part of the science he did. Eventually he wrote a great book, *Research Interviewing: Narrative and Context*, that I still recommend. He made a science out of listening to what people say and learning from it when you make room for them to say it in their own way. And, in fact, the science then did a better job figuring out and explaining a subject's world that the "instrument" was supposed to measure in the first place. He just needed a way to make himself and his subjects part of the research at the same time.

An Un-Reliable Science

Another difference that breaks a traditional science rule. Does all this self-reference and intersubjectivity and path dependence mean that two HSR projects might come up with different results? Yes, it practically guarantees it.

Think of two hypothetical HSR researchers. Say one is a Luo male from Kenya, to make it interesting in light of President Obama's ancestry, and the other is a female, half Chinese and half Anglo from Hawaii, to keep it interesting in light of where President Obama grew up, a "hapa haole" as they would say in the islands for him and her both. Both arrive in Washington, D.C., to do HSR research on how work is done in the White House.

Does anyone in their right mind believe that the two of them will come up with *exactly* the same paths of discovery and *exactly* the same conclusions, and that if they don't one of them has to be lying? Of course not. On the other hand, does anyone in their right mind believe that either of them can say whatever they want—"Well, that's just how I see it, take it or leave it. President Obama actually follows orders whispered to him through his iPod by Osama bin Laden, who is still alive in the White House basement where he plays Scrabble in Latin with Elvis." Of course not. Where's the evidence? Where's the logic? Where's the process of trying to prove it wrong?

More than one conclusion is possible, but not all conclusions are acceptable. That is the nature of path-dependent HSR. But the conclusions will occur within a space that limits the possibilities, a space whose boundaries consist of evidence, logic and falsification. Think about meteorology, like John Stuart Mill suggested. Weather is a *path*, the way different interacting variables link together over time and produce the changing weather on any particular day. But climate is a *space*, things like latitude and season and proximity to the ocean and mountains that limit the kinds of weather that might possibly occur. A particular HSR project is like the weather. It will finish with a careful documentation of its path over time and how it led to a Toulmin-like conclusion in the end. Then different projects within the same climate, metaphorically speaking, can compare different conclusions they reach, yielding a better understanding of the space within which possible paths occur. As we all know in 2013, with the exception of several in Congress, climate can change as well and change the shape of the space.

I like a skiing metaphor, it being winter as I write this with the ski mountain a few miles from my house challenging my work ethic. There are a potentially infinite number of possible paths down the mountain. "Runs" we would call them, each one a unique trail from the top of the chair lift down to Totemoff's for a bowl of green chile stew at the bottom. But there is also a mountain that limits where you can go.

The concept of "prediction" survives again, like it did in previous chapters. HSR can tell you about the space of possible paths and predict in that sense. But one particular research "run" will be different from another based on how all the interactions and contingencies play out for that particular project during that particular time.

Obviously an experiment can't allow any of this. If two scientists come up with different results, one or both of them have to be wrong. This makes some sense when the science is a science of *objects*, but not when it is a science of *subjects*. Different results in an intersubjective science mean an opportunity to learn more about the space that a human social world might travel, more about paths not taken and possible paths it might take in the future.

Writing the Results

Toulmin's diagram is a schema, a framework for a rational, self-conscious organization of knowledge that a researcher builds to make a credible case. A traditional experiment, as described earlier, is one way to use that schema, but it isn't the only way. With an experiment you can pretty much follow the Toulmin bouncing ball. Readers will probably have experienced the standard formats of most human social scientific articles. Hypothesis-research design-data collection-analysis-thank you very much. They are usually written up in a very linear way, not to mention boring to read. If they're not boring, reviewers get suspicious.

What does Toulmin have to say about how to translate his diagram into prose? Not much. He leaves it open.

In the late 1980s, a few anthropologists and sociologists, and probably people in other fields that I don't know about, questioned the sacred format for the journal article and the scholarly book and invited human social science to imagine new ways to write. I'm here to tell you that, on average, writing has improved, but the original revolutionary call went the way of most revolutions. The flywheels of traditional disciplines kept the old engine running in pretty much the same way.

Some colleagues left science and turned to art, literature, and film to express and evoke human social worlds whose intentionalities and lived experiences they had learned. There's much to be said for this. Artists have been doing that very thing at least since the cave paintings in El Castillo. I remember when I first started working with heroin addicts in New York in the early 1970s. In a previous chapter I mentioned a movie about addicts called *Panic in Needle Park*, screenplay by Joan Didion, one of Al Pacino's early roles. As far as conveying addict lived experience to a non-drug-addict audience, I felt like I might as well go home and hang up my field notes after I saw it.

Toulmin's model does help me avoid frustrated artist syndrome though. It draws a boundary around the science space and says, art is fine, but it does not have the characteristics of a science. No imperious judgment intended, just a fact, and I imagine most artists would agree. In art, there's no evidence organized by logic with attempts to falsify. That's not what bounds the space of possible representations of experience. I'm only a film fan and consumer, but it seems that you could use film to instantiate Toulmin, and then call it a "documentary." In fact, I've heard colleagues who do "ethnographic film" argue just this boundary, how much of their work is art, how much is science?

Toulmin does set limits—a space for the writing paths that research might take. He limits what kind of deathless prose can claim to be science. Within those limits, thanks to the work of those human social scientists in the 1980s, we know there are many more possibilities than traditional BSS and HSR templates used to allow for. The advantage of Toulmin, once again, is that his model opens things up on the question of how human social science can report the results of its work. It opens the space up because it doesn't dictate exactly how to do it. But it does tell you that, however you do it, certain criteria have to be met, the old litany, once again, of evidence, logic and falsification.

The writing can be fluid and show the researcher as part of the data. It can be organized in any number of ways, including the narrative style that became popular after the 1980s. Why not human social science as a mystery? Why not in the style of creative nonfiction? But in the end, if the research claims to make a scientific case about how the human social world works, the pieces of the Toulmin diagram need to be in there so the research can be evaluated by those who look to it for knowledge they can rely on.

Now, for the final Toulmin touch, I'd like to throw a logical changeup pitch into his diagram. This will take a fair amount of airtime, most of the next chapter. HSR learns as it goes, and learning logics look different from the deduction and induction that John Stuart Mill described. The fact that HSR is a different kind of science—the theme of this book—means that the "logic" part needs to be expanded. Since Mill's day it has been, dramatically so, especially since the creation and then boom in the use of computers to do intelligent tasks, a field known as artificial intelligence. That's where we'll go in the next chapter.

CHAPTER FIVE

The Heartbreak of Monotony

Return to the science chant that guides this book—evidence, logic, and falsification. A major question is, how can HSR actually use Toulmin's diagram to make good on the three requirements? Logic is the heart of it, like John Stuart Mill said, but he didn't go far enough to finish the job for HSR.

I'm no logic maven. In fact, I took formal logic the final quarter of my senior year in college, not a period in life known for its scholarly motivation. Not only that, it was 1967 in the San Francisco Bay area—bad timing for concentration. There were too many historically important distractions that defied simple logic, like civil rights and Vietnam. My friend Chris was the only person I knew who got an "A" in the course. And this was before grade inflation. He smoked marijuana before every test. Years later, after I became a drug expert, I still couldn't figure out how that might have worked.

Look again at the Toulmin diagram. The heart of it can be translated into the straightforward P implies Q of traditional logic, $P \rightarrow Q$, the "conditional" as it is usually called. "P" is the grounds, also called "reasons" or "evidence" in the diagram, the materials gathered and organized to support the claim. The grounds *imply* the claim. The grounds are where the hard labor is, clearing the rocks, weeding, plowing. It makes me think of the saying I learned when I painted a house—90% of it is preparation. Then there is Thomas Edison's less modest but more skewed version; genius is 1% inspiration and 99% perspiration.

The grounds get you to the claim, the "Q," when you make a case. *If* the grounds are true, *then* the claim is true. *If-Then*, another version of the classic P → Q of Logic 101. But why should anyone believe that those grounds imply that claim? Because the warrant says they do. And if you don't believe the warrant, there is another box right below it called the backing that explains why you should believe the warrant.

In Logic 101 there isn't much to discuss here. P → Q is a *proposition*. If the proposition is true, then that means that if you show that P is true, then Q has to be true. That is the warrant. And what's the backing? How dare you ask. It's a basic rule of logic handed down from the history of Western Civilization, developed in its modern form, like everything else in this book, starting in the 19th century.

With a real proposition, it's not just an abstract "P implies Q" anymore. P and Q mean something concrete and there's a reason you think you can claim that P → Q. That's what Toulmin learned from his teacher Wittgenstein. Nothing is ever only an abstract principle when it really happens. Why does P imply Q, for god's sake? What do people think about how the world works that makes the builder of a Toulmin case believe that his audience will agree that P → Q?

Is it a matter of the local version of "common sense" because both are investment bankers? See the recent film *Margin Call* if you want a terrifying glimpse of their version of common-sense in action. Or does the arrow rest on shared values because both are part of a pollster's demographic category, for example the category of "Hispanic" that played a central role in the 2012 presidential elections? Or is it a collective belief about what causes what, maybe that a full moon causes everyone in Podunk to drive like they're from New York City? Maybe it's even a cliché about the stock market based on gravity—"what goes up must come down"—Newton smiling in his grave at how physics can too be relevant to lived experience.

The point is, real-life warrants and backings aren't just abstract arrows shot through a logical vacuum. They grow out of intentionality and lived experience, just like the grounds and claims do. The logic has to be there; that part is true for any science. But its warrants and backings—they will be part of the human social world that has to be researched, learned, and then incorporated into the model. Toulmin guides us to put flesh and blood on those local arrows so that we can test them in a systematic way.

So far so good for the job of adapting logic to a Toulmin diagram. A researcher learns and gathers up the P's and Q's and the warrants that will link them together. At different stages she *induces*—where are the cases that show how P doesn't imply Q for example—and *deduces*—if P → Q is true what else might be true in the human social world that is the object of study? Her research will develop as the answers to those questions lead her to learn more and revise the grounds and claims and the warrants that justify them.

So who needs more logic than that? The problem is, something critical happens in HSR, namely, learning that changes the research even as it is being done. Isn't there a way to think about that conditional proposition so that it handles the learning and surprises that always come up? HSR needs more flavors of logic than John Stuart Mill provided. For example, in HSR, claims you wind up making, the "Q" in the conditional, are usually things that you didn't know existed when you first started the research.

A family of logics that can handle this—they would have given Aristotle apoplexy—is called *nonmonotonic*. The adjective looks like it means "not monotonous," and actually that's not so far from the truth. It means a logic where conclusions can change as more is learned. David Makinson, in his introduction to the field, points out that this kind of logic has been around for centuries. He wonders why the mainstream kept it on the logical margins so long. Amateurs like me would guess that that it was finally put on center stage only because the computer literati demanded it. If you're going to try and make a computer do something interesting, deduction and induction just aren't enough to get it invited to the right dinner parties. In fact, induction might insure that it would never be invited back again.

The artificial intelligence story pretty much parallels the BSS/HSR story I'm telling in this book. Early Enlightenment success followed by academic institutionalization locked in a way of thinking about logic going back to Aristotle's syllogism as the founding moment. In fact, John Stuart Mill was a radical innovator with respect to that tradition. But 20th century demands for new ways of representing thinking in a computer rattled the historical cages and new versions of logic broke out everywhere.

Writing about a research field that I think of as part of HSR, Makinson justifies the need for a nonmonotonic logic with this example:

> Archaeologists sifting through the debris of a site may see their early conclusions about the date, function and origin of an artifact change as more evidence comes to hand.

And then he described the logic more generally:

> In formal terms, we are said to be reasoning nonmonoton-
> ically when we allow that a conclusion that is well drawn
> from given information may need to be withdrawn when
> we come into possession of further information.

Nonmonotonic logic represents a dynamic learning process where things change depending on what just happened and what happens next. In other words, it is a path dependent logic that, at the same time, sets up the falsification that a science needs, only in a more dynamic way. It doesn't just say yes or no to a proposition. It can also say, you need a whole different proposition.

Toulmin's diagram easily absorbs this lesson. He didn't tell us how to do research step-by-step, not necessarily. He showed how to make a good case in the end, whatever kind of research we did. Smart computers and smart humans learn as they go, and what they learn changes early beliefs and conclusions into later ones, and those changes, in turn, change what the end of a project looks like compared to what was imagined when it first started.

P's still imply Q's—"mind your Ps and Qs" isn't a bad mantra here—but they and their warrants and backings move and change with experience, namely, the lived experience of a researcher doing research as he learns about the lived experience of subjects in their ordinary lives.

There are several types of nonmonotonic logic. If you remember Leon Festinger's famous concept of cognitive dissonance, described in the second chapter, you might guess that one version is called *belief revision*. You thought the world was going to end? It didn't. Another example is *default logic*. For example, nonmonotonic logicians are fascinated with penguins for some reason. All birds fly, you say? Meet a penguin. But "all birds fly" remains the *default*, because it usually works in the absence of a few items of specific information that are unusual, like that you live in the Antarctic, or have just seen the movie *Happy Feet*.

For now, I want to look at just one type of nonmonotonic logic, called *abduction*, and talk a little more about how it works. I've written about it before, as have other HSR types. This logic has a pedigree going back—here we go again—to the 19th century, only this time it's an American instead of a German who cultivated this peculiar P and Q strain.

Where Do New Ideas Come From?

Charles Peirce (1839-1914) was a genius with a bad reputation. William James credited him with the creation of American pragmatism – that was the genius part. Bertrand Russell, another genius with a bad reputation, called him the greatest American thinker ever. Peirce worked at numerous jobs, an appointment at Johns Hopkins University being his main academic position. But then he took up with a mysterious woman named Juliette, and he did it before his wife left him. The Stanford Online Encyclopedia adds to the intrigue by claiming that she was a gypsy. Another source claims she was only French, not quite as exotic, but mysterious enough. The resulting scandal got him fired.

He was apparently a difficult person, at least in part because of illness, and he made enemies easily. But he also had supporters, like William James, who organized a fund that kept him from complete poverty for a while. In the end, though, he died destitute, leaving behind 12,000 printed pages of work and 80,000 pages of handwritten material. He may have been an obnoxious libertine by the standards of his day—it's hard to know without diving into his and her biographies in a serious way—but he was a genius, no one disagrees with that.

Right now I want to use him as an innovator in this P → Q logic business, an innovator of extreme value to HSR, not to mention to the modern field of artificial intelligence. Pierce created something called *abductive* logic. Many people—especially residents of Roswell, New Mexico, think of abduction in connection with "alien." In Roswell, in the summer of 1947, so goes the story, an alien craft landed in the desert, where it was captured, concealed and denied by the U.S. government. Roswell still has a UFO festival every summer. One day I want to sip an espresso at the *Not of This World* Coffee House.

Abductive logic is a little different, less dramatic than an alien kidnapping, but more realistic, and it does "take a person away" from how they were thinking before they used it. The concept mutated a bit over the years in Peirce's own work and it has shape-shifted among a few contemporary HSR types as well. A famous academic article compares Peirce and Sherlock Holmes. Sherlock mentions his powers of "deduction" here and there in the many mysteries that Arthur Conan Doyle wrote. Sherlock was often technically incorrect. Often he was *abducting*, not deducting, much like an HSR researcher does.

The resemblance between HSR and detective work is fun to play with. In fact, before I teach an HSR workshop, I ask participants to watch an old Colombo TV episode and read a mystery novel to get them in the mood to think abductively when they arrive. Take a break from this book and watch Colombo on the Internet or rent a DVD. I know, I'm showing my age again, but Colombo reminds me more of cops I knew in my drug research days than do the slicker versions on TV now. "Cops love Colombo," several cops told me over the years. And it amazes me that usually young people and international audiences know of the show, even today.

Watch how Colombo works. The show opens with the crime, so we, the viewers, know the *real* Q right away. Then he rolls up in his old Peugeot with his half-smoked cigar. Everyone, including the cops, thinks the Q is something else because of the clever way the murderer set it up to deceive them. You see Colombo figuring out that the "obvious" Q isn't the real Q, usually from the way that the criminal acts in the face of this dumb non-threatening detective, a master of intersubjective navigation. "I apologize for interrupting a person as important as you" and "Oh, and just one more thing" appear early in the show. The drama—and the fun— of the show is watching Colombo, whom everyone thinks is a little dim, figure out the real Q and, along the way, the P that implies it. By the end, he is all of a sudden not the bumbling idiot that the murderer initially took him to be, but the accuser with a Toulmin diagram so tightly wrapped that the murderer confesses.

As a Detroit detective put it—he took a workshop I taught at the University of Michigan—"We work alike, but in the end you say 'I get it' and I say 'I gotcha.'" Colombo taught me more about HSR methodology than any of my courses, which is easy to say, because, in my student days, there weren't any courses that taught HSR methodology.

A researcher might *think* she knows the Q at the beginning, like everyone in the opening scene of a Colombo episode, and she might be right, but she needs to check and make sure, because there's an even greater chance that her initial assumptions about the Qs that matter and the Ps that imply them are wrong. In fact, based on experience, the smart money will bet that a researcher will be surprised at how different subject lived experience and intentionality are compared with what she assumed at the beginning of a project. The Q will be a surprise and the P and the arrow that connects them will take her to places she didn't know existed when a project first started.

Try writing that in a research proposal for NIH or NSF, or in a methodology section of an article for a BSS journal, if your self-esteem can take it.

An Abductive Parable

Here's an example of how abduction works in an HSR project. Years ago I worked with independent truck drivers. They were called "independent" because they owned and operated their own trucks. Media at the time idolized them as the last of the American cowboys, out there, alone on the Interstate range, hauling freight rather than driving cattle, making it or breaking it, come what may.

I spent time working with them, travelling with them, hanging out with them and their families, and listening to their stories to see what their lived experience was like. Mostly what I heard about and saw was *dependence*, not independence. "Independent" truckers depended on companies for their contracts, their freight and their paperwork, on shippers and customers for loading and unloading, on a labyrinth of federal and state agencies for their right of way. "Q," their lived experience, was more about being a dependent trucker than an independent one. So what was the "P?" It sure wasn't going to be an intentionality based on independence, because independence wasn't what their lived experience looked like at all.

The Q I expected didn't work out. So my book, *Independents Declared*, pretty much "de-glamorized" the independent trucker in a way that the men and women I got to know actually liked.

They were annoyed, as it turned out, that their public image was the mythic free-wheeling cowboy when the real issues they dealt with weren't even on the radar screen of the big shots in business and government on whom they depended—that word again—to make a living.

I wound up building a book around a Toulmin-like argument that showed the grounds, the P, for claiming that so-called independent truckers were really dependent truckers. First I had to change the Q; then I had to go looking for new Ps that implied it according to some warrants and backings. The heart of the entire project was a very large *abduction,* with many smaller ones included in it. The Ps I needed weren't hard to find. As one trucking company owner summed it up after he heard a talk I gave, independent truckers were the "serfs" of the trucking industry.

But then a fascinating twist came along while I was gathering up the material to make the case—and "rebut" and "qualify" it, if you recall those boxes in Toulmin's diagram. It turned out there *was* a kind of independence. But it had to do with the time and space coordinates of work, not with autonomy from the social and economic ties that the rest of us depend on.

The independents didn't work an eight hour shift and a five day week like most working people. "Truck time," as I called it, was made up of a trip that had a beginning and an end, but the trip hardly ever mapped neatly onto the clock and the calendar. And then "truck space" was the entire United States, punctuated with "truck stops" where you could sleep and eat and talk to anyone you met about trucking in ways that an outsider wouldn't understand. As far as the normal time/space coordinates of ordinary working life went, a trucker who owned and operated his or her own rig was, in fact, independent of the usual nine to five schedules and specific workplace locations that most of us deal with.

Then again, this was before the Internet linked on-board computers with corporate headquarters, so things are probably different now.

After the book came out, a trucker sent me a poem about how trucking was like Einstein's theory of relativity. Montie Tak, the author, had been an English major before going into trucking and had written a truck dictionary called *Truck Talk* that I used as a resource. What she wrote in the poem was that the time/space dimension moved around with you and your truck at the center. I was grateful. It was a nice piece of evidence to decorate the final Toulmin conclusions.

How does this trucking example illustrate the importance of abductive logic? The project started with me, the researcher, having the idea that P → Q meant that owning your own truck made you an "independent" trucker. Wrong, at least as I, the researcher initially thought about it. And wrong, as it turned out, the way several truckers I talked with first thought about it, too. Several told stories about how they bought a truck in a "take this job and shove it" moment to spring free of factory or office work, but then they went into shock when they learned how dependent they were and how little money they made when it came to the bottom line.

Owning one's own truck meant that Q was actually a "dependent trucker." That was the surprise I had to deal with, a new version of their lived experience I hadn't expected. So what was the P that explained *dependent* trucking? This kind of change is the heart of HSR abduction, an *unexpected example of lived experience, a Q, that you have to figure out how to describe and explain from a first person point of view, the P*. Much of the P—not all of it— came from what I learned about the beliefs, desires, feelings and purposes of independent truckers.

Abduction is a nonmonotonic logic for learning. The Ps and

Qs and arrows change to accommodate revisions based on what has been learned at each point during the research. Answering the unexpected question about dependence was the main part of the book I eventually wrote. It made a case along Toulmin lines that described and explained the web of dependencies in which the so-called independents worked, a web over which they had little control.

But then I did find something that looked like "independence." And that discovery in fact resulted from following John Stuart Mill's advice to go forth and dig up negative cases. "Independence" meant the autonomy of the work in time and space compared with most jobs, whether your collar was white or blue. Maybe the original Q was right after all, but it meant something different in trucker lived experience from what I had expected. And a more complicated P explained it. It wasn't just about owning your own truck, though obviously you had to have one. It was about how *you* were the one who picked when and where to drive it. Well, within limits, like a promised delivery time and a customer in a specific location. But still, it was a far piece from the time clock right inside the employee's entrance.

So the HSR story went like this: Start with P → Q. It turns out that subject lived experience isn't the Q you expected. So look for the new Ps that imply the revised Q. But then it turns out that there is a different version of that original Q after all in subject lived experience. So then where is the P that implies that? It's messier than the Colombo scenario, but then real human social worlds are more complicated than TV show plot structures.

This abductive cycle is critical for HSR, because researcher and researched lived experience and intentionality are *never identical*. They might even be worlds apart, even though they might be expressed with similar words and grammar. There will always be surprises. Abduction, along with its other nonmonotonic kin, is the logic suited to this kind of research journey. It is a logic that requires a *translation* between researcher and subject as part of the science, a connection that is lacking in most of BSS, a missing ingredient that makes it look so distant from the world that it is supposedly about. That topic, translation, will be a centerpiece of the next chapter.

In the end, the independent trucking research plunged me into some personal epiphanies based on self-reference as well. I dispatched trucks as a part-time job when I was in high school. My cousin was a Teamster. As I started the study I realized that the truckers and their families were the people I'd known when I was a kid. I was using the study to try and combine my personal past with my professional researcher present. It worked out pretty well, too.

An even more powerful blast of self-reference occurred when I talked about the research in Sweden. Students and colleagues seemed to enjoy the presentation, but then they kept asking me about "independence," what did it really mean, where was the theory of it? I bumbled and stumbled for awhile and then realized—and told them as I became aware of it—that my basic drive to look at independence was personal, nothing to do with theory at all. The "independent" truckers were like me, angry at a contradiction between what American ideology told them to be and what American institutions made it difficult to do. We were all malcontents, me and my subjects, for much the same reason. The Swedes didn't have this problem, so they assumed it was a theoretical question, not a personal one.

None of that self-reference got in the way of the science. It did make it more passionate and personal, even before I knew what it was, but that just meant I cared more about what I was doing. More on this level of self-reference when we get to Milgram's obedience experiments in Chapter Seven.

Abduction in Action

Abduction—and other nonmonotonic logics—fit the bill for HSR. They allow for surprises and creation and revision. Learning where new concepts come from was one of Peirce's main interests. He noticed that deduction and induction were *closed* with reference to the concepts used by a researcher. With deduction it's obvious. You start with the premises already in place. With induction it's a little more subtle. You notice X and Y, but the noticing is based on what you're already predisposed to see. In both cases, a researcher brings concepts into the science that were already in place, ready to wear, salient, as the psychologists like to say. Not with abduction. It's designed for learning something new, for reacting creatively to something you didn't expect.

I should add, for those who want to pursue this concept later, that Peirce and others offer some definitions of abduction that are more tightly wrapped than the version that I'm about to present. An example is in the chapter notes. Some versions used by the artificial intelligentsia, for example, are more bound by available concepts. I picked the Peirce quote I'm about to cite for obvious reasons—it captures a key characteristic, and a key strength, of HSR.

Abduction, the way I'm using it here, is about a *creative reaction to a surprise*. It is a logic that engages the unexpected and creates new concepts to imply it. Here's one summary of how it works, in Peirce's own words, though I'll write P and Q in place of the letters he used:

> The surprising fact, Q, is observed.
> If P were true, Q would be a matter of course.
> Hence, there is reason to suspect that P is true.

Over the years I've called these surprises that the logic labels with a Q *rich points*. That concept started out with the notion of a "breakdown" from the philosopher Heidegger, as in his example, you don't know what a hammer is until it breaks, then all of a sudden you know what you don't have. The rich point phrase caught on for a while. The ultimate compliment came when a colleague in a related field who will go unnamed actually stole it. That person announced it as his own discovery in lectures in Europe, one of whose audience members told me about it. I was honored.

Rich points always come up in HSR. All the term means is that something surprising happens that catches a researcher's attention. The reason it is "rich"—whatever words or actions it might refer to—is because it usually signals differences in lived experience and intentionality between researcher and subject. HSR, more often than not, winds up focusing on rich points by the end of a project. The independent trucker research, and pretty much every other example I've used in this book—they all have as part of their story a surprise that appeared shortly after a project started that became a focus of it by the end.

Abduction flags a major problem if you're about to write a proposal for a BSS dominated review panel, which most of them are. An HSR researcher can always tell you how he will start a project. And he can tell you what he will do *next* at any given moment during a project, but only at that moment, not before the fact. Anything else he tells you before the project starts, it will be his best effort to write for a BSS audience who want a fully specified three to five year plan in advance. The irony is that the plan never works out anyway. I joke that an HSR researcher has to lie to write a proposal for mainstream funding agencies. It's a joke because there's truth to it, not "lie" with intent to deceive, but rather "lie" as forced to look enough like BSS to get funded.

Then again, HSR isn't *all* surprises. Once an HSR researcher has had his abductive epiphany, it's time for the old-time religion, deduction and induction. Peirce said the same thing. Once you abduct your way into a new P → Q, you switch on John Stuart Mill's Method of Joint Agreement and Difference machine and look for more cases with not P and not Q to fill in the other boxes of Mill's induction diagram, if a reader recalls that diagram from Chapter Two. And that's not all. Starting with that new abducted P → Q, you also deduce other things that should be true given the new proposition and look for them as well.

The key to understanding this dance of the different logics is that *abduction produces a proposition*. But then from a new proposition you can *deduce* another. And, starting with that new proposition, you also look at additional cases as they come along, positive and negative, and *induce* until the money runs out. In what I like to call the *logical trifecta*, abduction produces a proposition, deduction spells out its consequences, and induction looks for cases where it doesn't work.

Here's an example of a deduction from the project with independent truckers: A rich point, a surprising Q right in the beginning, was their complaint about dependence on a trucking company in order to get a load of freight. A few older truckers mentioned some government decision in the 1950s that they had heard of. I *deduced* that the decision was a major event that would help explain the complaints I was hearing. So I hunted down records of the decision in the archives. The result? An amazing story of how trucking was re-configured after World War II to the independent trucker's disadvantage. Not only that, but it was an example of how those without lobbyists at a Washington hearing get the short end of the stick, that being the most polite way I can think of putting it.

And *induction*? I was always looking for negative cases to complicate a proposition that I'd abducted. I often joke that an HSR researcher is an ambulatory falsification machine. For example, after awhile I wondered if there weren't some way to be an independent trucker, some way that resembled the media image of the last of the open-range cowboys. One legal way was to haul raw agricultural products, an exemption from the post-World War II hearings thanks to agricultural interests. But more exotic still, I found another way. It was called "hot freight," which meant exactly what it sounds like, illegal goods and illegal deliveries. I spent some time at a hot freight center during the project once I learned about it. Cash, no questions asked, back roads all the way, and a lot more money for the independent. Cowboy desperados in living color.

Abduction is a logic that handles the trial and error and imagination and uncertainty of HSR science, some of the reasons that HSR is so stimulating and so difficult to do—not to mention so anxiety-provoking for graduate students when they start their first project. But when an unknown world of subject lived experience and intentionality is both the starting point *and* the descriptive and explanatory goal of the science, you just can't do research without abduction. You can't learn and document another point of view if you control subjects by keeping them locked inside your own design. You can be sure there will be differences between researcher third-person and subject first-person points of view, but you can't be sure of what those differences will be until you go to work and find them. You might not like them—you might even find them immoral—but you have to know what they are rather than what you assumed them to be before a project started.

The most important propositions in the Toulmin-like case that an HSR researcher builds will start life with abduction, or with other nonmonotonic logics, not with deduction or induction.

Deduction and induction, as the examples I've described show, don't vanish in HSR, far from it. In fact, without them HSR can't be a science. For BSS, on the other hand, abduction is an object of fear and loathing, not to mention a career spoiler. Abduction derails the hermetically sealed linear sequence of steps and the illusion of control that BSS relies on to support its claim to be a science, not to mention the assumptions about who the subjects are that get challenged the minute you open up a two way conversation. Abduction puts intersubjective learning and creativity into the science even as it is being done.

Toulmin's model is fine with this. You use his model to keep an eye on what you need to learn, go to work, and you say to yourself, "The Q? Wait for it." It always shows up sooner or later.

HSR Logic

Let me go back through this chapter and put the pieces together. A rich point, a surprise, something that doesn't make sense, triggers abduction. Abductive logic and its nonmonotonic kin provide a framework to organize unexpected rich points and a guess about intentions and lived experience that might imply them. The abduction, in fact, is a proposed *translation* between two different human social worlds, a topic that will fill the next chapter. And it guides the creation of a Toulmin diagram to clarify and then test the rational reconstructions that a researcher builds.

A researcher imagines what he would do in the same circumstances, or, to put it another way, in the context of that kind of lived experience. He imagines this based on all the evidence available at that moment. *If* that were true in my life, thinks the case-maker, *then* I might do this as well. At first the odds are good that he will get it wrong and have to go back and revise it. And the Toulmin diagram, just as in the previous chapter, provides a model for the science, the critical organization of evidence and logic that can then be falsified in any number of ways, the more the better.

This summary is intersubjective all the way up and all the way down. Rich points come out of researcher/subject encounters that make differences visible. But underneath the clean diagrams and formal logics are the conditions that make human understanding possible at all. Dilthey used the German word "verstehen" to summarize them, a word usually translated with "understanding" in English. We are able to make up a rational reconstruction to translate differences because we, the researchers, can imagine what another human social world might be like. This basic human ability is called *empathy*. It is a universal part of intentionality and lived experience that makes rational reconstruction possible at all.

Empathy isn't just an emotional "I feel your pain," as President Clinton used to say, though it can be that. And it's not just "Feel me?" as in, "Do you understand what I mean?" like Omar used to say all the time in episodes of *The Wire*, though it can be that, too. It is a universal ability that humans develop around the age of four, an ability that enables them to know that another person has a model of the world different from theirs because of that other person's different lived experience.

Remember how Mill worried about making humanity's natural ability at induction into a science, because humans had another natural ability, ways to eliminate cognitive dissonance, that worked against it? The problem with empathy runs in parallel. A human ability, one of which—empathy—makes a science possible, conflicts with another human ability—naïve realism—that gets in the way of its use. The solution? As Mill argued, we need a logic to get from the natural ability to the science. For empathy, the logic is abduction, as developed by Peirce and the nonmonotonic artificial intelligentsia.

It really is amazing to think of how humans are naturally predisposed, at one and the same time, *both* to science *and* to anti-science.

Abductive logic isn't as crisp as Mill's induction, though as we saw in Chapter Two, his logic unraveled a fair amount. But the abductive variety does block the naive realism that tends to dismiss a surprise as an error, a mistake, or a deficiency on the part of the humans who produced it. Naive realism has to be tranquilized so that a surprising difference in lived experience inspires some new ideas about what intentionalities might explain it.

Abduction, driven by that mix of evidence and empathy, is where the human social science action is. And I mean "action" in two ways, first because it guides analysis of the phenomenon that the science is about—human subjects in their social world—and second because it is the place where the researcher starts converting experience into an HSR science framework.

In the next chapter, I want to dive into this space where researcher and subject actually meet. It is where the presence of researcher as part of the research becomes obvious, where she learns and then includes subject intentionality and lived experience on the way to making a case, where she organizes the results to respect scientific demands for evidence, logic and falsification, and where she relies on an empathy based on human universals to translate the results.

The space is full of motions and sounds, and marks on paper, and many other sensations for that matter. How can a researcher engage that sensory soup to learn the intentionality and lived experience that it expresses and then change his or her own assumptions about the world to make sense of it? What does a researcher focus on to figure out his or her third person account of a subject's first person view on the way to a first person plural rational reconstruction? And then how can a researcher craft a translation between an audience and the subjects that the researcher has learned to describe and explain? How does a researcher not only make a case, but also make it in a way that connects different human social worlds and includes them all in the conclusion?

That's where the next chapter needs to go. We'll start with the differences and wind up with the universals that make it possible to make sense of them. We'll use the notion of translation to mix the UP—universal person, the LP—local person, and the OP— the own person all into the same research conclusion.

CHAPTER SIX

When Researcher Meets Subject

At some point in human social research, researcher and researched deal with each other. It might be face-to-face, like in an interview or experiment or fieldwork. It might be one step removed from the researcher, like a hired assistant. It might be one step removed from the research subject, like archival or digital records. Whatever the case, the moment of contact will have a *context* and it will *mean* something. To oversimplify, but not by too much, it will have a context based on lived experience, and it will mean something in terms of intentionality. The problem, as I've mentioned several times already, is that there will always be differences between researcher and subject in lived experience and intentionality, whether they are in direct contact or not.

"Contact" sounds a little too dramatic, like a scene from the movie *Cowboys and Aliens*. Let's call such moments an "intersubjective space," in keeping with the intersubjective nature of the science and the nonlinear dynamic idea of a space of possibilities. It means human social science on the ground, in real time, when a researcher looks at, listens to, or talks with a human research subject, or looks at the trail that subjects leave or objects they make, whether those trails and objects are physical or archival or

155

digital or anything else. It also means the space shared with audiences for the research, with colleagues or clients or funders or the subjects themselves, anyone who wants to know the results.

For any two people, there will be some differences in lived experience and intentionality. That means that, however trivial or profound they might be, there will always be differences in meaning and context when those two people communicate. The dilemma for human social science of whatever type is: How can a researcher find out what the differences are, then translate them, then figure out if they matter for the connection between science and subject worlds?

In this chapter I will use the terms "meaning" and "context" for the way intentionality and lived experience take shape at a particular time in a particular space. Intentionality and lived experience are the lumbering all-inclusive German philosophical terms, the cargo ships. Meaning and context are right here and right now, the jet skis. In this chapter, we'll leave the ship channel and explore the harbor and get a little wet.

The "M" and "C" Words

Most readers won't have run across terms like "intentionality" and "lived experience" before reading this book. But with "meaning" and "context" it's a different story. Think for a minute how often you have used or heard those two loaded terms as signals that something went wrong.

"That's not what I meant at all."

"You're taking my words out of context."

Or think of them in a more positive light.

"Let me explain what I mean."

"A little context will help."

How often do you hear or say these kinds of things? All the time. Such expressions surface frequently because glitches, usually trivial, sometimes funny, now and then life threatening, appear in the intersubjective space among people, whether face-to-face or distant in time and space.

And the glitches don't just appear in words, either. Not so long ago, I met a filmmaker and he asked me to look at a short video on his computer. "What did you think?" he asked. I told him there were parts I didn't understand. "Ah yes," he said, nodding and smiling, "This is a film of many secrets." I asked how I was supposed to get it if it was full of secrets. He looked at me like the pathetic victim of Hollywood that I am and left to find a more interesting conversation.

Even a statistical table from the census—what do the numbers *mean* and how can they be put into some kind of *context*? That table, too, is the end product of intersubjective spaces, even though it is a researcher looking at some numbers. The human subjects on the other side of the researcher are far removed in a long sequence, though. First, someone filled out a form at the kitchen table, or else they talked with someone at the front door. That completed form, and many others, went into a computer programmed by someone in an office. Someone else organized the output into categories. An office full of people wrote the results into reports. A university library reformatted the material in a different way and a professor and graduate student published an article. Someone decided that the journal would go into a database. And finally, another researcher printed out the article that started long before with people filling out forms at their kitchen tables. This is an intersubjective space with a long chain of people in it. It, too, is a film of many secrets.

But the fact that the chain is hidden from the researcher reading the article doesn't mean that meanings and contexts weren't translated along the way. The translations aren't always easy. One famous census problem at the moment is, what kind of boxes does the government offer for people to indicate their social identity and what do the box(es) they select mean? Is there a box for President Obama to check that says "Luo-American?"

Sometimes the differences that fill an intersubjective space can get pretty funny. When I was drafting this section of the book in the community college library, I took a break and walked over to the gym. Two guys were talking. One said, "How's the new station coming along?" "Good," said the other, "we're figuring the coverage area now." "What's it going to cover?" asked the first guy. Then the other listed some towns to the south of Santa Fe.

In order to avoid exercising, I chimed in, "What kind of programming you going to have?" "Programming?" he asked, like it made no sense at all. "Yeah," I said, "You know, what kind of music you gonna play?" "Whatever they want to," he said. We stared at each other, both trying to figure out what was going on. His eyes lit up and he grinned. "It's a *fire* station," he said.

On the ground floor of any project, the researcher and the researched make "data" together in those intersubjective spaces. "Data" is just a name for what is understood and recorded from a researcher's point of view. The space might even be a document about an event that happened 100 years ago. There were still subjects back in there somewhere. They mean or meant something in *their* contexts, and a researcher means something in hers. The trick is getting the translation between the two right so that the language of the human social science has some correspondence with the intentionality and lived experience of the human research subjects in their social world. Otherwise—I keep asking—what is the science about?

BSS simplifies "data collection" by assuming that the contexts and meanings of research are understood by subjects in the way that the researcher intends, and that there will be no differences among subjects as to how they interpret them. HSR, on the other hand, assumes that researcher and researched meanings and contexts will be different—different between researcher and researched, and different among those being researched—and that this is a problem to attend to.

Not only a "problem." More interesting still, it is a source of data, because the "problems" mean that something different is going on in subjects' worlds that a researcher didn't expect. Sometimes it's a trivial difference that doesn't much matter. Sometimes it's a spectacular rich point and an HSR researcher is happy about the whole thing and abducts away. At the other extreme, it might be a difference that means nothing gets done, the wrong things get done, or maybe that the subjects shoot the researcher or, worse, call their lawyer.

Meaning and context are my favorite parts of HSR. Remember Rutherford, the annoying physicist quoted in Chapter Two who thought it all boiled down to physics? The truth is I'm just as bad. I think it all boils down to intersubjective translation. Meaning and context are where intentionality surfaces in lived experience and works its magic. They provide the content that fills a Toulmin diagram and guides HSR into a rational reconstruction of subjects that, in turn, starts the journey towards the science. They are the meeting ground for the "subjects" in the "intersubjective."

Learning, and then working out the translation among meanings and contexts in the space where human social science actually happens, this is the antidote to the problem of ecological validity, described back in Chapter Two, namely the question of what human social science results have to do with human social reality.

It pushes exactly that question right down into data collection rather than delaying it until later, after the results come in. Attention to meanings and contexts in the intersubjective space brings both points of view—researcher and researched—into the science, right from the start. It's not just us, and it's not just them. It's how we translate those different human social worlds to make the data for a human social science together.

Language

Intersubjective space is built out of human communication. That obvious fact signals the relevance of a number of academic and practical fields that are more—way more—than I can cover here. Readers who are seriously bilingual/bicultural will know from personal experience the many differences that go into switching from one language to another. Not just words and sentences, obviously, but jokes, idioms, entire ways of speaking, mentality, not to mention all the other symbols through which meaning and context are conveyed—body language, intonation, clothing, physical distance, and the list goes on.

I debated whether to dive into this topic at all during different revisions of the book. It's an overwhelming job to contemplate, partly because it's the area of HSR in which I've done the most work. The first decision I made was to restrict the broad range of communication to the more narrow topic of language, obviously a central part, but not the whole story. We language addicts often talk about how, to most people most of the time, language is just an obvious way of passing information back and forth, no problem, nothing to pay attention to there. Language is much, much more than this. We like to say that we want to make language the visible or audible surface of rich meanings and contexts of the moment, a surface that in turn represents the intentionalities and lived experiences of the speaker or writer.

In this section I'm just going to introduce a few key features of language—how central a part it is of being human, how powerful a system it is, how it guarantees differences in the intersubjective space of research. The overview will be too fast and too light, but the topic needs some mention in a book about a different kind of human social research. A major reason a different science is required is because humans have language and the minds and societies that go with it.

In the 1990s I wrote a book, *Language Shock: Understanding the Culture of Conversation.* It isn't a bad introduction to HSR style language research, if I do say so. In that book I used a made-up word, "languaculture," meant to remind readers that speaking and lived experience and intentionality come together in a package when people communicate. The concept, colleagues tell me, helped change fields like second language instruction and intercultural communication. It even made it into Wikipedia, and I didn't write the entry. But enough about me. I will use "languaculture" now and then in this chapter as shorthand for "language/meaning/context" in the same breath.

There are three main points to make here. First, if we look at language origins we see a major evolutionary event that made humans what they are today. But, second, that event also made human social science the different kind of research that it is, because it guaranteed communication differences that the science would have to handle. And third, those same differences raise the ecological validity question, because the language of the science and the language of the human social world have to be translated into each other if the former is to have anything to do with the latter.

Spoken human language relies on *sound symbols* that have no necessary relationship to what they mean. "Cat," to honor our pet Waldo, has no necessary relationship to the animal that the sound refers to. The sound sequence does not *point* to an animal. It does not *resemble* it in some way. It is a *conventional* tie between a string of sounds that mean nothing and something in the world that means a great deal. This separation of sound and meaning gives language its spectacular power to represent and communicate an infinite number of things.

Where did this ability come from? Many are the arguments and speculations. Certainly the development of Broca's and Wernicke's areas in the brain played a crucial role, as did the enlargement of the brain more generally. The L-shaped vocal tract, so goes another argument, gradually evolved starting with bipedalism. Speculation now flourishes that mutation in the FOXP2 gene may have something to do with it, though the jury's still out on that one. As one would expect, however language emerged, it was made up of many interacting factors. Evolution, too, is a nonlinear dynamic system. In this business there are no simple causes.

One thing is clear though, at least as of today: The descent of the larynx—the phrase sounds like a sci-fi thriller or a gothic computer game—played a crucial role. Like everything else in human evolution, that assertion is no longer the simple fact it pretended to be. But the lowered larynx allowed humans to produce a virtually infinite number of symbols by stringing together relatively few distinct sounds in multiple ways. The descended larynx enabled a symbolic combinatorial explosion.

No longer did a particular sound have a particular meaning, like an alarm cry meaning danger. Now sounds coupled with meanings in an arbitrary way. "Arbitrary," in fact, is a so-called *design feature* of human language. The separation of the sound system from the meaning system also has a name. It is called "duality of patterning." Two independent patterns, one made of sound units, the other made of meaning, link together in arbitrary ways.

And the new symbolic system could represent events separate from when they actually happened. This ability also acquired a special name. Linguists call this design feature "displacement"— language can represent entities distant in space and time —a logical term suggesting as it does that time/space coordinates of speaking can be separate from when the thing spoken about actually occurred. Language can also slice and dice a meaning into finer parts and produce the sounds to communicate them. This feature is called "productivity." Productivity means language can create new symbols as the need arises.

Charles Hockett, the linguist who first described these design features, argued that duality of patterning, displacement, and productivity were the three features that best distinguished human language from other communication systems in nature. But how did this ability get harnessed to meaning and context? The experts say that human thought and social communication showed signs of life well before Homo sapiens sapiens became the meaningful sound-spitting creature that it is today. Merlin Donald, one well-known theorist of language emergence, says that, "language, including speech, had started to evolve much earlier than 50,000 years ago," that being one estimate of the date when modern humans are said to have appeared in their full cultural glory.

Donald speculates that a middle stage between early hominids and the culture explosion might fill in the gap. Homo erectus, the ancestor to modern humans, must have been capable of some communication that went beyond animal systems. Their brain size increased considerably, up to 80% of later Homo sapiens sapiens volume. They migrated out of Africa and populated Europe and

Asia, and they dealt with harsh and frequently changing climates. They used fire and cooked food and developed new tool kits. Homo erectus didn't change much over their long run, from about one and a half million to two hundred thousand years ago. But still, they must have developed communication beyond the abilities of the primates.

Donald describes what he calls a "mimetic" culture that might have been intermediate between the episodic culture of animals and early hominids and the culture with a capital "C" that came later. "Episodic" refers to episodic memory, an ability that animals have as well. Remember Waldo the cat? He was more than just a reaction to the sound of a can opener. But he certainly was that as well, and a reaction to a can opener is a perfect example. Episodic memories activate when a simple cue, or a few of them, occur in the world and register on the animal's sense receptors. There is a direct link between perception and memory of a sequence of things to do. But there is no sense of a self separate from the episode nor is there much if any remembering or imagining of the episode absent the cues that actually trigger it.

Mimetic culture, Donald thinks, was a system of communication that went beyond the episodic moment and set up conditions for human language to come. A major achievement of mimetic culture was what he called "autocueing," which means that a memory could be called up and communicated separately from when the situation itself actually occurred, an early form of displacement. In linguistic jargon, this was an advance from an "indexical" to an "iconic" sign.

Indexical, in this context, means you point to the thing you want to refer to. Something has to be within perceptual range and then you can nod or point to indicate that what's going on represents what you mean. Iconic, on the other hand, means a symbol

164

that has some kind of *resemblance* to what it refers to. One can communicate without the actual object or person or event that one wants to communicate about actually being present. Flapping your arms suggests a bird. A ritual dance suggests a hunt because one dancer wears an animal skin and another carries a weapon. A throwing motion with an empty hand suggests an actual toss of a spear. Note that this is prior to the stage where arbitrary sounds, like "cat," can represent an animal. A sign with a resemblance to a cat might be a meow-like noise.

A second change with mimetic culture, according to Donaldson, was a shift away from what he calls "cognitive egocentricity," in other words, a shift towards an ability to think of a task separate from one's own involvement in it. This was the beginning of a sense of self separate from immediate experience, crucial for the eventual development of human language, not to mention a sense of lived experience. One can't contemplate the world unless one stands apart from it.

Those developments—autocueing, iconic communication and a separate sense of self—distinguished mimetic culture from the episodic culture of animals and early hominids. I think Donald's speculation makes a lot of sense. Human language didn't come from nowhere. And, as he argues, modern humans still use episodic and mimetic skills. They are part and parcel of our inheritance from animals and our ancestors.

Mimetic culture names the development of increasingly sophisticated abilities to communicate. In retrospect we can look at it and see human languaculture coming—or think we can—as primates led to early humans led to Homo sapiens sapiens. In the end, Homo sapiens sapiens developed an extraordinarily powerful ability—human language—which they could use to communicate about virtually anything. The ability blossomed with a combinatorial explosion where language, contexts and meanings could be put together and expressed in conventional and arbitrary ways. Within a human social world, this made life more sophisticated and socially intricate than had ever been possible before. But *between* human social worlds, the conventional and arbitrary ways that meaning and context got tied to sounds, and later writing, were never the same. A human researcher of human social worlds can never assume that his languaculture will be heard and understood and responded to in the ways—many of them out of his awareness—that he expects.

Translation

Fascinating a topic as contemporary debates around the origin of language might be, we return now to HSR. Language evolution is only meant here as a backstory. The important thing that an HSR epistemology has to deal with are the consequences. Languacultures of research and subject worlds will *never* match perfectly. Translation is always required. If it isn't done, then the research is condemned to ecological validity hell. Differences in meaning and context will be obvious when researcher and subject languages are noticeably different, like English and Mandarin. It gets more subtle, less visible, but equally important when researcher and subject speak the *same* language.

For example, when I worked with heroin addicts in 1968, it was my first HSR research in my own language. It didn't take long for differences to appear, even though we were all speaking English. "Square," for addicts, meant a person who didn't use heroin. That's all it meant. In my English, it meant a person who hummed along with the music when riding in an elevator. A more serious example: In psychiatry-speak "paranoid" meant suspicious to an irrational degree. But in the dog-eat-dog street world, one survived by continually worrying about others' intentionalities. It wasn't irrational. So-called paranoia was actually street-smart.

In the end, focusing on meaning/context differences, even among speakers of the same language, helped me learn how addict intentionality and lived experience were different from that of "squares." The *same* words could represent *different* meanings, and the different contexts in which the language was used explained why they were there. By paying attention to and translating those differences, I gathered up material to fill in a Toulmin-like diagram for a science of addict intentionality and lived experience. In the end, HSR helped explain—with cases like "paranoid" versus "street smart"—how and why "treatment" didn't work, and why most BSS research on addicts hadn't noticed that they were anything other than social psychological failures. Naïve realism shaped most of the human social science about them.

Here's another example of how differences come up in the same language. The easiest project I ever did was the one with independent truckers, mentioned in the previous chapter. They were the adult versions of the people I went to high school with. Ordinary language was no problem, since I'd grown up with pretty much the same American English dialect. But the language relevant to the work of trucking was dense with meanings and contexts I'd never heard before, even though it was in English. I had to learn them before I could function in the intersubjective spaces of the project at all. Same conclusion as the addict research: The meaning/context differences in the "same" language were the portal into the intentionality and lived experience of other speakers of it.

One quick example: The simple English word "cowboy." At the time I did the research, popular media were full of images of the "independent" trucker as the "last of the American cowboys," the mythical figure used by so many to symbolize what we think of as our national character. As I learned trucker languaculture, though, it turned out "cowboy" meant a reckless unprofessional driver, a negative description, not a positive one. That difference in meaning and context spoke volumes about how most independents disliked, even hated, the popular use made of them, because the popular image trivialized their own struggles to survive economically during the early 1980s.

Those are only two examples. Differences in meaning and context always surface, even if researcher and researched speak the same language. An intersubjective science has to take this seriously. A rational reconstruction based only on the meanings and contexts of a researcher will never get it right. If you're a researcher, and your own personal languaculture hasn't broadened by the end of a research project, you're in for an acute attack of ecological *in*-validity, guaranteed.

With this simple fact—that human social science is at base an encounter between at least two partially different systems of meaning and context, two different languacultures—we land on the ground floor of HSR, look around, and see again how different it is in fundamental ways from the ground floor of the BSS tradition. That tradition *controls* the communication based on researcher intentionality and lived experience, researcher meanings and contexts. Subject languaculture is allowed into the intersubjective space only to the extent permitted by the scientist's research design. Rigid adherence to researcher languaculture kills subject languaculture softly with its song instead of using it as a path into their intentionality and lived experience.

Getting From Here To There

How does a researcher carry different languacultures from that intersubjective space to a final presentation?

You have to start somewhere. To climb out of that space with some data, a researcher has to work out a *translation* that connects the different languacultures in play. A translation straightens out the communication, whether in the "same" language or between different ones. It isn't a one-step process. Translation happens when researcher and subject interact. It also happens when a researcher converts what happened into "data." It happens again when the data are represented in some kind of form, like a Toulmin diagram, and again when a final report is created for some audience. A good translation has to carry subject worlds all the way from their everyday expression into a researcher's description and explanation of them in a scientific format.

Here's an example. Years ago I worked with Herbert Huncke, a heroin addict elder in the streets of New York. Huncke was the famous street connection for the Beat Scene that developed after World War II. He is "Elmo Hassel" in Jack Kerouac's *On the Road* and "Herman" in William Burrough's novel *Junkie*. We worked together on his life history for a year and a half in the 1970s.

Huncke and I would meet in different places and talk informally. One time he described sitting in a train station during the winter. I later learned that this description translated as a sign that things weren't going well in terms of his hustles or his friends, that the location where he sat was part of a survival map for a homeless person in cold weather. Later I transcribed his words and then used the transcript to look at the story he told about how he learned to be a burglar. The railroad station was actually a set-up for the story, because the desperate conditions in his life meant he was disposed to take the risks of trying out a new illegal activity. Later, my colleague Jerry Hobbs and I looked at the transcript using a logic resembling the logics described in the previous chapter. We translated some of Huncke's story into that logic to make explicit the patterns that we saw in his language. After that we wrote the results in a style suitable for an academic audience.

Here's an example: At one point in the hour-long story, Huncke talks about selling stolen goods in a cafeteria. He walks over to the table where the "fence"—the buyer of illegal goods—sits with two young guys. Many things are said. Among them, Huncke says to the kids that they're making a "general display" of themselves. The place is "loaded with rats" or police informants. The "whole table" will get busted if they don't quiet down. We then used Hobbs' nonmonotonic logic to make clear how the display would *enable* the rats to *cause* a bust. We called this kind of link among utterances "local coherence."

This logic/content mixture—drawing attention and avoiding arrest—happened all the time in the interview in many different ways. We called this "thematic" coherence. So we created a general schema for the theme from which all these specific instances could be derived, a schema that showed how "avoiding attention" was part of a continual worry in the life of a street addict, since so much of what they did involved activities for which one could be arrested. Specifically in this story, it helped explain Huncke's worries about learning a new hustle, namely, that he didn't know it well enough to avoid attention when he did it. We called this schema an example of "global coherence," since it was relevant to so many parts of this particular interview, and most of the other interviews as well. Not to mention what I saw all the time in the streets.

The many steps in translation began in the intersubjective space—me and Huncke talking in his friend's apartment. They continued with a translation for and then collaboration with my colleague and ended up with an article for an audience of cognitive science academics. These steps were, in fact, part of the *grounds* on which we made our *claim* about Huncke's life, to use the language of Toulmin's diagram. We concluded with a rational reconstruction that showed how junkie lived experience relied on an intentionality organized around keeping a low profile to avoid arrest, in a context of heroin dependency and in an environment that made arrest more immediately threatening than a non-addicted bourgeois audience had ever suspected it could be. Recall the description of the use of "paranoid" earlier in this chapter—namely, that continual suspicion was "paranoid tendencies" from a clinical viewpoint, but it was "street smart" from an addict's point of view—and you see why this difference was worth reporting.

Translation started inside the intersubjective space and continued all the way to the published article. It served to align researcher meaning and context with meanings and contexts of subjects, colleagues and audiences. By the end, the researcher had more control over the presentation than the subject did, true enough. On the other hand, in this particular case, Huncke took the transcript and published it himself in a literary magazine. He didn't give me any credit for editing it for him, either. The point for now is this: Translation made the science intersubjective all the way through. The space of the original encounter that made the "data" was intersubjective, and so was the space of the resulting science.

Translation as Intersubjective Science

Human social science has much to learn from *translators* and *interpreters*, those unsung heroes who work to make communication across languacultural differences possible for us all. Over the last few decades they have come out of their traditional self-effacing closet, as they should have long ago, since their work is difficult beyond anything that the monolinguals who rely on them can imagine.

Let me use a little translation jargon for an introduction to what happens in the intersubjective space. The translation field speaks of the *source language* or SL and the *target language* or TL. I add another element and use SLC and TLC for "source languaculture" and "target languaculture." The concept of languaculture recognizes that two people speaking the "same" language might be using very different meanings/contexts, or that two people speaking "different" languages might be using very similar ones. There are fascinating complexities in translation given our contemporary global society that I'm neglecting here.

The goal of HSR is to learn to translate from a source—that of subjects—into a target—that of an audience. No one that I've read, from any field, thinks that translation involves a simple one-to-one transfer from source to target. Even a simple translation, like "dog," varies dangerously when its meanings and contexts are looked at. In the jargon of translation studies, a perfect *equivalence* between SLC and TLC is simply not possible. Either source, or target, or both, have to be bent and molded and shaped to accommodate each other. If the source is shaped to better fit the target, then the translation is said to be "domesticated." On the other hand, if the target is shaped to accommodate the source, then the translation is said to be "foreignized."

Remember the Schmäh concept from Austria back in Chapter Three? Recall how much work it took to get its first person meaning and contexts right from my third person American English point of view? Some dictionaries and writings and conversations translated Schmäh into English as "joke." That was domestication with a vengeance, a way to make the concept easy—but also inaccurate—for English speakers. What I did was to foreignize the concept for English speakers to pull them toward an Austrian first person point of view, in the deeper sense of Schmäh, that "irony" was the best way to make it through the day.

The problem is this: The target community is usually paying the translator, and that same target might well dominate the source, politically and linguistically. So the tendency is to domesticate the translation in the direction of the target to make it easy on *them*. In the case of BSS, the target—the traditional science community—requires target dominance as part of the scientific method.

HSR, in contrast, wants to foreignize the most critical differences between researcher and subjects to foreground the previously unknown parts of a subject world for a target audience. The point is to give bring outsiders closer to a sense of the lives of research subjects.

One of my favorite articles of all time illustrates how this connecting tissue starts to grow. Laura Bohannon, working with the Tiv in Nigeria during her fieldwork back in the 1950s was asked to tell a story from her world. She picked Shakespeare's *Hamlet*. During her telling of *Hamlet, the* elders felt they had to correct the story, because parts of the story made no sense to them. For instance, of course the slain King's brother married his wife right away. It was the proper thing to do, what a Tiv man would do if his brother died, not the scandalous act interpreted by Western audiences. In her self-deprecating humorous style, Bohannon shows how her Tiv audience *domesticated* Hamlet for Tiv consumption.

But there's another way to read her article, a preview of where this chapter is going. How could the Tiv understand anything, and how could she understand the corrections and the reasons they were making them? And then how could she tell us, her English speaking audience, how it happened from both points of view? The *human universal* ties between her and the Tiv and her audience made it possible to write the article for us, and for the Tiv to find Hamlet comprehensible and yet at the same time to "correct" it, and for us, the audience, to enjoy her amusing adventure in the intersubjective space of the research from both her and the Tiv's point of view.

A 16th century play, narrated by a 20th century American anthropologist, did in fact make a lot of sense to senior members of a—at the time—isolated Nigerian tribe. (Now of course the Tiv have their own web pages.) The sense made by the Tiv was different, but different in recognizable ways to us once Bohannon worked her way up the levels of translation from the story-telling moment to her article.

Bohannon wrote to display differences. But the differences and the universals actually mixed, moment-by-moment. The Universal Person and Local Person and Own Person blend again in the rational reconstruction, if the reader recalls the "a person is like all others, some others, and no other" quote in Chapter Three. This blend of universal, local and idiosyncratic is the secret to connecting different languacultures in an intersubjective space. Pay attention to the differences that come up, but then figure out how they can be translated in terms of human universals. That universal base allows a researcher to first learn, then later to foreignize the translation just enough so that an audience understands important differences in meaning and context between their world and that of research subjects. And vice-versa, the translation back into subject worlds being a neglected possibility in much human social science work.

Crossing a Languaculture Canyon

I'm guessing most readers will agree, especially those with personal experience of living in two languacultures, that translation is possible, come what may. Some parts of the job are easy. Some parts are difficult. Some are major challenges verging on the impossible. Laura Bohannon gave us an idea of how it works. Who can tell us how it happens in a little more detail? Especially the near impossible parts, which more often than not are signals of important differences—rich points—between human social worlds?

Think of the example of Schmäh from Austria again. That was a tough translation, but it finally boiled down to irony, a universal concept if there ever was one, and irony made translation from Austrian German to American English possible. Here's another well-known example, from Catherine Lutz, a colleague in anthropology who figured out words for emotions in the language of the Ifaluk, a people who live on a coral atoll in Micronesia.

Rather than looking for English translations, she introduces and then continues to use native terms, like I did with Schmäh. Then she takes the English-speaking reader into descriptions of real situations that the term labels. Lutz uses English to give an initial idea about an Ifaluk concept, but also, more importantly, to show the reader how the English term is related but at the same time doesn›t really fit. X (in Ifaluk) is sort of a mix of A, B and C (in English). So we—the English speaking readers—get a rough idea of the translation, but also an idea of why a word-for-word translation can't work. Then we learn what the term does mean as she shows us case after case of Ifaluk lived experience where the term applies until we «get» it. The Ifaluk emotion concept is eventually foreignized for us. For example, we finally understand the word "fago" as a mix of love, compassion and sadness. And, if you don't recognize that emotional mix, you haven't listened to any country/western music in awhile, that being my youthful California Valley version of many other genres, like Blues, Corrido, Rembetika, Fado, and I'll stop there, even though I'll bet the Ifaluk have their own fago-themed songs.

This is a classic HSR strategy. Its general goal is to foreignize important differences in lived experience and then show an audience how to understand the difference by stretching their own intentionality and lived experience so that, in the end, they understand something powerful and important about the people who live in a human social world different from theirs.

But translating means, once you've figured out the difficult connections, like going from "fago" in Ifaluk into English, how do you explain them, either Ifaluk to English, or English to Ifaluk? Where is the connecting tissue of shared humanity, the universal human intentionality and lived experience that you find wherever you go? Where is the universal *ground* against which the *figure* of foreignized translation becomes possible at all?

The Space Between

That universal part of intersubjective space—translation theory loves to talk about it. Concepts have sprouted like tropical plants in a rain forest. Whatever it is that goes on in there, it is what makes translation possible at all. Those of us who rely on it—whether we're researchers or globe-wandering backpackers or international travelers or political refugees or transnational CEO's looking for a country with lower tax rates— that universal part makes it possible to find common ground, with any luck with pleasant and useful and entertaining results.

Exact equivalence in translation is not possible. But even major differences in meaning and context can be translated. How can both of those things be true, because both of them are?

Bassnett, in her frequently cited classic that blends local differences and human universals, points out that it is an "established fact" that a dozen translators working on the same poem will produce a dozen different translations. But then she writes:

> ...somewhere in those dozen versions there will be what Popovič calls the 'invariant core' of the original poem. This invariant core, he claims, is represented by stable, basic and constant semantic elements in the text, whose existence can be proved...

Whatever it is that happens in that universal space between langua-cultures, more than one translation is possible, but not any translation is acceptable.

Remember the discussion earlier about nonlinearity and the multiple paths it allows? Bassnett says that translation in particular, like HSR in general, is a nonlinear dynamic system. There is a space that limits the possibilities, but within that space there are a number of paths that a translator can take. Remember when I was trying to translate Dilthey's concept of "Geisteswissenschaft" back in Chapter Three? "Geist" sort of meant this and "Wissen" sort of meant that and "schaft" made it an abstraction. I didn't say it at the time, but within the space of possible translations "HSR" looked like one option, but it certainly wasn't the only one. That's how it goes whenever the translation is interesting, interesting in the sense that it signals the kind of rich point that always flares up in language when differences between human social worlds appear.

Rubel and Rossman, in their introduction to a recent collection of essays on translation, write something similar. "… foreign texts are seen as entities with invariants, capable of reduction to precisely defined units, levels and categories of language and textuality." But they also write that many researchers have a serious problem with this idea of universals, because universals might well wash out attention to local specifics and encourage the naïve realism of the target audience.

Human social science needs to find the right balance here. We've returned again to the UP, universal person, and LP/OP, local person and own person, discussion from Chapter Three. Obviously everything in a particular moment of human social life isn't unique. Obviously some of it generalizes to a social identity. And obviously everything isn't a universal. Which is which and how do we weave them together into a rational reconstruction that does the science job without distorting the meanings and contexts of human subjects or of the science beyond repair? The universal similarities are as important as the local differences. The dangerous part, as said several times in the book already, is the line between an appreciation of human universals, on the one hand, and naive realism, on the other.

Here's an example of how tricky this can get. A few years ago some American development types who worked in China invited me to coffee in return for some free advice. They—all Anglo-Americans—were having a "cultural problem" with one particular Chinese individual. They'd read my book *Language Shock* and thought maybe I could solve it for them. They figured that any problem involving an American and a Chinese had to be cultural. I listened to their story.

"What if the person is just a pain to deal with?" I asked. It was a little impolite, but then it was meant to shock them. They did look at me like the proverbial deer in the headlights. Was I an ultra-nationalist naive realist disguised as a culturally sensitive expert?

So I elaborated. Did they have similar problems with other local people? Did other local people working on the project see the person in question as a pain, too? Nothing more than a list of improvised John Stuart Mill type questions in a hunt for more cases to fill the empty inductive logic diagram from Chapter Two.

They talked some and decided no and yes, in that order. Then I asked them, did they act like Americans are often said to act in international settings, arrogant and dictatorial, getting away with it only because of the money the victims couldn't have unless they went along with the game? No, of course not. Well, they allowed, maybe they could have included him more in their planning conversations in the evening at the NGO bar and grill. So maybe he wasn't spilling over with team spirit because he wasn't treated as a team member?

The coffee talk wasn't science, but they did pick up the tab.

How "cultural" was their problem? Everywhere in the world I've ever gone, short visit or long term stay, there have been people who strive for historical significance by making as much of what anyone else is trying to do as difficult as possible. Differences in LP/OP norms exist, no question about that. Some places it's normal to be blunt; some places it's normal to be politely indirect. But with those local norms as anchor points, there are always a few people who go to extremes to make life painful. The development workers' Chinese colleague might have been a classic universal example of the former, a pain to deal with, recognizable by anyone, anywhere, compared with other locals.

On the other hand, maybe the Chinese colleague was angry about the Anglo-American crew rolling in and treating him, the local program director, like a personal shopper. Maybe he knew that their imported plans were—not only naïve—but destructive of the very goals they meant to achieve. Maybe he decided to go along to get the money, but he wasn't about to admire and respect them for their arrogance and naivete. Everywhere I've gone in the world, I've seen "resistance," as the social theory jargon likes to call it, the universal ability of people to accept a situation when power dictates no other choice, but to display their attitude even while following orders.

So now the DC colleagues had two plausible reasons why the "cultural problem" might not have had much to do with "culture" at all.

Some things are true about people everywhere. I call this personal folk wisdom the *soap opera principle*. People who enjoy international travel or work well in foreign lands intuitively apply it all the time. The name for the principle came to mind one day when I checked into yet another hotel in yet another place I knew almost nothing about and turned on the TV. A soap opera was playing. Everywhere I went there were soap operas, and I could look at any of them and recognize a fair amount of what was going on.

I sometimes think of my first days in an isolated South Indian village when I was a junior in college. I remember what a strange mix of feelings it was, the heavy dose of culture shock at the differences, but at the same time the comfort from immediately understanding many things people were doing around me. In those days, we anthropology students were told to go after the differences. But it was the universals that made it possible to notice the differences at all, and then start to figure them out, and eventually come home and describe them and explain how they made sense.

I think this is where human social science has its most interesting theories, right at the intersection of the universal human situation and the histories that shape particular human lives. In the description of Brentano's work in Chapter Three, Jürgen Habermas was quoted. It makes sense to repeat that quote here.

> When the pre-theoretical knowledge to be reconstructed expresses a universal capability, a general cognitive, linguistic, or interactive competence (or sub-competence), then what begins as an explication of meaning aims at the reconstruction of species competencies.

The missing theory of human universals is the great void in human social science today. The topic was taboo in the past in anthropology. In fact, some still see *any* proposal for universals as naive realism, arrogance, or a power play, period. And of course such proposed universals can be exactly that, and often have been. Universals are extraordinarily dangerous territory. It is right to worry that an important difference will be "domesticated" just to keep the audience, not to mention the researcher, comfortably nestled in their home-grown meanings and contexts.

The danger requires precautions. One precaution is the careful construction and clear understanding of just what counts as a human universal and what doesn't. We don't have that clear understanding. But at least in recent times we know we need it and work is underway in several disciplines. We know that human universals are real. And we know that they can be assumed and abused in service of naïve realism. Those propositions define another cutting edge problem, as I revise this chapter in 2013, for human social science.

An Example of Universal Progress: An Anthropologist's Epiphany

Donald Brown tells the story of his human universal epiphany in a bizarre high tech setting. You can see the brief video on the web— the URL is in the chapter notes— and I highly recommend that you watch it. In the video, he looks like someone I might run into at my high school reunion, older, white, wearing a V-neck sweater over a dress shirt. He got famous back in 1991 when his book, *Human Universals*, was first published. He's become the required citation for any of us who want to talk about them, and he deserves to be.

Like me, he was trained as a cultural anthropologist. Like me, his training aimed him directly at cultural differences. Anthropology's message to the world was: The "People of Village X" aren't like us, but that doesn't mean they are more primitive or, worse yet, moral degenerates. Their culture has its own integrity and consistency and complexity. It is just different, that's all. So now let me tell you about those differences and why they make sense.

In those days we were crusaders out to conquer the barbaric naive realists. That was anthropology's mission. There were plenty of them around. There still are. We taught class after class of undergraduates, and said, over and over again, that each human, each group, each culture was different and had to be understood in its own terms. Ruth Benedict, author of *Patterns of Culture,* probably the best selling anthropology book of all times, wrote about the "great arc" from which each group selected the pieces of its culture. The fact that there was a great arc implied a limited number of universal possibilities, but neither she nor the rest of us who read her book talked about that.

What about those things in her book that were *not* different, things that made a connection between Anglo readers and Native American research subjects possible? When Benedict talked about "Appolonian" and "Dionysian" native cultures in her book, we American readers had a general idea of what she meant without a lot of elaboration on her part. How was that possible? Were those universal yardsticks she used to make sense of North American Indians like the Kwakiutl and the Hopi the right ones to base a translation on, or did they distort the two Indian worlds to make it easy on the English speaking reader? I mean, one of the first things I learned when I moved to New Mexico was the story of the Pueblo Indian revolt of 1680. The Hopi, along with other Pueblo groups, killed the priests, razed the churches, and drove the Spanish back to El Paso. Was that Appolonian, "characterized by clarity, harmony, and restraint" according to the dictionary? It was certainly "clarity," from a Pueblo point of view, but "harmony" and "restraint?"

Most BSS type human social sciences had—and have—the opposite problem. They usually don't worry about "cultural differences" much at all. They assume they are working on universals. That assumption is obviously doomed as well. Differences *do* matter.

Psychology is one of the worst offenders. Joseph Henrich's 2009 review article criticized psychology for using samples drawn mostly from the WEIRD, the *W*hite *E*ducated from *I*ndustrial *R*ich *D*emocratic countries, mostly college undergraduates. He and his co-authors showed that, when you compared the results of psychological research on the WEIRD with the much smaller amount of research done among the non-WEIRD, it turned out that the non-WEIRD samples produced very different results. WEIRD research couldn't just be assumed to be research on humans in general. It was research on the WEIRD, period. The question of what was universal needed more work.

Universals have been a neglected problem for years, whether they have been ignored, as in anthropology, or assumed, as in psychology. Obviously both need to be included in HSR, from epistemology all the way down to translation in the intersubjective space of research.

The Universal Person

Donald Brown has developed his ideas about human universals considerably since his 1991 book. But in that early work he has a chapter where he sums up some universals by describing a *Universal Person* or *UP*, the same acronym I've already used in the book. I want to excerpt just a part of his description, a description of all of us, to give a flavor of some of the things a theory of universals has to describe and explain. What follows will give a reader an idea of the many universals in play when two humans meet.

The Universal Person has a language, and being good at using it is well regarded. Gossip is important, as is humor and the ability to deceive others. The UP's language uses sounds found in other languages. It also contains nouns and verbs, subjects and predicates and objects in some order, as well as figurative speech like metaphor. UP's language will always cover certain semantic territory, like color and kinship terms, body parts, natural phenomena, emotion, time, and many other things. It will be used to tell stories and sing songs and recite poems.

UP will use a logic with relations like part-whole and kind-of and implication and negation. Facial expressions and intonation will express some emotions in a universally recognizable way. There will be a concept of "person" with responsibility for actions and intentionality. Sexual attraction and jealousy will be part of life. UP will make and use tools of certain types, like cutters and pounders and levers.

UP will have a family. There will be ways to prepare for a birth and then rites of passage for life events like marriage and death. An incest taboo will prevent marriage among certain relatives. UP will recognize a division of labor based on sex and age, and those same age/sex differences will be relevant to many other areas of life. There will be status differences and an unequal distribution of wealth and prestige. A government with leaders will be present, and some system of laws/sanctions will exist. Laws will always regulate violence and rape and murder.

There will be a strong sense of an in-group/out-group boundary but also value placed on etiquette and hospitality. Empathy and envy will be present and there will be standards of modesty. A religion with supernatural beliefs will offer magic and ritual and explanations of events like disease and death. A system of hygiene will be part of life and there will be aesthetic standards. A "triangular awareness" will be present, which means an ability to think about relationships of two people with each other separate from one's own relationship with them individually.

Brown's book contains many more universals, a discussion of the research on which his UP is based, and the fact that "universal" doesn't always mean the same thing. Some universals, for example, are rooted in the biology of the human species while others look to be more experiential. Still others are widely distributed but not quite universal. Brown concludes his chapter on the UP with a summary of how anthropology has neglected the topic:

> In sum, a fuller and truer account of the UP would in various ways show the relationships between the universals. … Anthropology has scarcely begun to illuminate the architecture of human universals. It is time to get on with the task.

As of today there is still no overall theory of human social universals. But more research on specifics is underway than I've ever seen in my lifetime. It shows how testing universals offers potential collaborations between HSR and BSS, a collaboration that will be the centerpiece of the next chapter when we look at Stanley Milgram's obedience research.

When Is a Theory Not a Theory?

Universals make translation of differences possible, and without translation there can be no intersubjective human social science.

There is a story to tell here about grand old man of anthropology Robert Redfield. Right after World War II he wrote an article about how the Rockefeller Foundation asked some human social scientists to look at the very best work in their various fields and figure out what it was that made them great. It turned out the answer was not methodology, which is what everyone expected. By and large the best of them broke the methodological rules of their home disciplines. Remember *When Prophecy Fails* by Leon Festinger? Classic case in point.

What made them great, Redfield wrote in his article, was a way of looking at a particular moment of the human situation in terms of what the moment said about humanity in general. It was the link, abductively produced, between what he called "*the eternal and the ephemeral*" that made for outstanding work. In this sense, Redfield added, great human social science had more in common with great literature than it did with any particular methodology, BSS or HSR or any other. That "eternal" space is why the Tiv could understand Hamlet even as they corrected it. It is my "soap opera" principle.

As Donald Brown said in the quote cited earlier, it's high time we all get on with the job of developing a theory of who we are. The more modest point for this book, to repeat the theme yet again, is to show how HSR is a different kind of science. The "behavior" that becomes the "data" of the science is for the most part located in an intersubjective space where researcher(s) meet subject(s). The space is made up of languacultures, systems of meanings and contexts, and a researcher cannot assume at the outset that he knows what, if anything, subject systems look like from the subjects' points of view. BSS solves the problem by requiring subjects to adapt to a languaculture pre-structured by the researcher in the name of scientific control. HSR works out a translation between researcher and subject so that the translation, which includes them both, will make up a good part of the material that goes into a rational reconstruction.

That translation—I'll say it once more because it is so important—is not possible without a universal human base in terms of which a translation can be forged.

Whatever else it does—so argues this book—human social science has to be about subject intentionality and lived experience. To do otherwise would be like a physicist saying you can go ahead and ignore mass and motion. Getting from subject intentionality and lived experience to a human social science means that translation becomes a core part of the science, that much of what happens on the way to a Toulmin diagram is the use of translation to make a claim that subject worlds can be represented in a rational reconstruction in a particular way. It don't mean a thing if it ain't got that languaculture swing.

CHAPTER SEVEN

Human Social Science

As far as I'm concerned, my main mission is finished. The *Lively Science*, a coarse-grained satellite image of HSR, is complete. There is much, much more to talk about, but it would bloat the book beyond a newcomer's desire for a first look at the territory. Now that I've reached this point, I should probably quit. But I want to develop two themes from previous chapters, the first, how HSR and BSS can work together in the quest for human universals, the second, how the political and historical context of human social research shapes its space of possible paths, self-reference writ large.

This book has already used examples of BSS research and interpreted them through HSR eyes. To take a more detailed look at how the blend can work, I want to dive into one of the most famous BSS studies ever, the experiments on obedience to authority conducted by Stanley Milgram. He was a disciplinary maverick with research relevant to the Holocaust, so his work backlights all sorts of issues about how a project is linked to its times.

I had him in mind when I first thought about this book a couple of years ago, because I wanted to challenge my own description of the limits of BSS with research that I admire and consider one of the most important contributions ever to academic and popular knowledge about humanity. The funny thing about the choice, discovered after I made it, was that a good biography of Milgram had been written by Thomas Blass. The title of the next section is the title of his book and, if what you read here is of interest, I highly recommend it. It turns out that Milgram was more HSR than I expected.

So I'll start in on those twin issues—the potential of BSS work for HSR and the importance of the researcher's biography and historical era—both of which come together neatly in the story of Stanley Milgram.

The Man Who Shocked the World

Stanley Milgram (1933-1984) was a social psychologist who pioneered studies on obedience, social networks, and urban life, among many other things. Lucky for me, I found Blass's 2004 biography, *The Man Who Shocked the World: The Life and Legacy of Stanley Milgram*. This section uses a few anecdotes that he described. Learning new fragments of Milgram's life and work led me to appreciate how he, like Festinger with his cognitive dissonance, followed many of the guidelines that in this book have been called HSR.

Milgram also serves as an example of how BSS moves to center stage when universals are at stake, and universals—as the last chapter showed—are essential for HSR. HSR can of course propose them and challenge them. I will do that with Milgram's work later in this chapter. But when it comes down to a claim that a specific human intentionality or lived experience is something that is part of being human, then it is time for an experiment, one that should hold up everywhere, with everyone. And if it does hold up, and continues to do so, the results contribute in turn back into a theory of universals, the very foundation that makes HSR intersubjective work possible at all. The potential for this conversation is spectacular, as Donald Brown said in the previous chapter.

It's a "love and marriage go together like a horse and carriage" kind of thing. Or maybe better, as men and women used to joke about each other all the time in my youth, "can't get along with 'em, can't get along without 'em."

Milgram was a genius. I'm only using the first project that made him famous here—the experiments on "obedience to authority." In that research Milgram showed that ordinary people, when instructed to do so by an experimenter in a laboratory-like setting, would throw a series of switches that they believed sent severe electric shocks into a person who, as time went on, hysterically demanded release from the study and then went silent at the end, a person who had mentioned a possible heart condition before the study began. In the original version—more detail to come—26 out of 40 subjects, or 65%, went through the sequence of switches in the "learning experiment," all the way up to the maximum of what they believed to be a 450-volt shock. And they gave the silent "victim" three jolts of that before the experiment was declared over.

As it turned out, Milgram had displayed HSR tendencies in his life and his work long before the obedience study. For his dissertation he had decided to test Asch's famous experiments on conformity—an Internet search will tell you what you need to know about them if they're new to you. They have to do with how powerful "peer pressure" can be. Milgram decided to run similar experiments in other countries to see if the results varied. With the exception of work in anthropology, this was a pretty radical thing to do back in the 1950s.

He obviously knew his way around languacultural differences. Blass' biography describes in several places how internationally oriented he was. His French was so proficient that when he appeared on television in that country people assumed he was French. In both France and Norway he used his experience with local language and culture to make sense out of his research. In Norway, for example, he learned that his preconceptions about "Norwegian individualism" were way off the mark. He had expected *less* conformity in his experiments when compared to the U.S. Not true. He explained his mistake with the nationally known custom that Norwegians called "Jante Laws." One law said "Thou shalt not believe thyself better than us." Not exactly solid HSR science, but heading in the right direction.

Where did Milgram's HSR proclivities develop? I don't know, but Blass offers several anecdotes in the course of his book that show it surfacing here and there. A particularly striking one comes from stories told at a memorial service in New York after Milgram's death. Roger Brown, faculty member at Harvard during Milgram's graduate student days, described how Milgram handled seminar assignments:

> Instead of leading yet another bookish discussion, he brought in an audio tape he had made of many kinds of psycholinguistic phenomena: slips of the tongue, rhetorical flourishes, a child's first few words, a stretch of psychotic speech, all wittily edited and assembled and presented to us as things to be appreciated first and then, perhaps, explained. And the only reading course I remember was the one with Stanley on crowd behavior in which he did no reading at all for some time, but, instead, went all over Boston joining crowds of every kind and

> bringing back snapshots of curious group formations. (pg. 21—page numbers refer to Blass's book.)

Milgram got away with this—in Roger Brown's case was even appreciated for it— because he had the good fortune to be a graduate student in an experimental program at Harvard called SocRel, short for "social relations." That program was founded in 1946 to continue the transdisciplinary collaboration of different human social scientists that developed during World War II. It consisted of social anthropology, sociology, social psychology, and clinical psychology. This is an odd and interesting mix, including one field built on HSR (anthropology) and another with an HSR subfield tucked away in it (sociology). The program ended in 1970 when the sociologists quit. Postwar euphoria couldn't last forever. A published description in the *American Psychologist* in 1946 described SocRel like this:

> While [academic] departmental lines have remained rigid, there has been developing during the last decade, a synthesis of socio-cultural and psychological sciences that is widely recognized within the academic world in spite of the fact that there is no commonly accepted name to designate the synthesis (pg. 18).

Apparently no one had read Dilthey, or maybe the term "Geisteswissenschaft" didn't have the desired rhetorical impact in English language administrative memos.

Milgram was a graduate student in the SocRel program during its heyday. He was curious about how the human social world worked, in general, not just as understood in his particular chosen specialty of social psychology. As Roger Brown's stories suggest, he tended to go out in the world and look around before he did an experiment. His ability at living in a foreign language in a foreign place shows that he understood languaculture and how to handle it. He trained in transdisciplinary human social science. Theory and hypothesis, as understood in the mainstream of BSS, made no sense to him as the primary way to organize a research project. These are all characteristics of HSR as I've described it in this book.

But he did do laboratory experiments and he did them well. The way he did them also foregrounds some HSR attitudes, reflecting a controversy still alive and well in social psychology and its modern variants. Milgram designed experiments in an HSR kind of way. By that, I mean the experiment wasn't built on top of odd-looking tasks that had no relationship to situations in a subject's world. Rather, it was designed to recreate and dramatize *real* situations that could conceivably be part of a subject's *real* lived experience.

What an interesting compromise, this kind of experiment, a mix of BSS laboratory isolation and HSR engagement with subject lived experience. Milgram's laboratory was apparently *not* artificial for most subjects; it was like a realistic film scene. The approach is called "experimental realism," according to Blass, the creation of a situation "that is so compelling and involving for the participants that they cannot respond with rational detachment, thereby increasing the validity of the findings" (pg. 260). This is close to achieving that elusive oxymoron, an "ecologically valid experiment."

Milgram was no stranger to the arts, including film and TV, both for his own use in his research and with others who used his experimental results to artistic ends. As Blass writes:

> He saw a close affinity between the experiment and theater. He expressed this idea almost aphoristically:

"Good experiments, like good drama, embody verities."
... In his experiments, Milgram was much like a director
of a play, both in his meticulous attention to technical
details and staging and in their intended effects on his
audience (i.e., readers of his reports) (pg. 263).

Shades of Redfield's comparison of great human social science
with great literature, mentioned in the previous chapter, where he
said that the criterion of greatness for both was a universal human
theme dressed in local color.

So where is the boundary here? An experiment becomes real?
Or, looking at it in the other direction, reality offers a "natural
experiment?" The setting itself, and the reactions of subjects as the
experiment progressed, are described in dramatic and eerie detail
in Blass' book. A search on YouTube will show a reader many
different videos of the experiment, if you want to get a visual sense
of how it might have felt to have been a subject. This blurring of
world and experiment fires the imagination with ways to think
about HSR/BSS collaborations.

The Experiment

Here is Milgram's original design. The subject walks into the room
with another person whom he thinks is just another volunteer. Actually the other person is part of the research team. The two draw slips
of paper to determine who will be the "teacher" Both slips of course
say "teacher" to make sure the subject gets that role. The "learner"—
remember, he's part of the research team—goes into another room
where he can only be heard but not seen. The teacher is instructed

195

to read pairs of words and then read one word from that list. The "learner" must respond with the correct paired term. If he does *not* get it right, the teacher will give him what he believes to be an electric shock. With each new mistake, the teacher increases the voltage. It starts low at 45 volts but escalates in steps to 450 volts at the maximum. Remember, no actual shocks are given to the learner.

The machinery for administering the shock, as I just mentioned, was created with all the care of a set designer. It had clearly marked switches for voltage amount. The teacher is given a real sample shock of 45 volts before the study starts, which he—they were all "he's"—typically estimates as much stronger than that. When the experimenter pressed the switch to start the experiment,

> ...the machine sprang to life, like a stalking cat whose prey had finally come within his reach: The light above the switch turned bright red, accompanied by an electric buzzing sound. The flashing blue light labeled "voltage energizer" was activated, the dial on the "voltage meter" swung to the right, and the relay clicks sounded (pg. 85).

Even though a majority of teacher/subjects went all the way to maximum voltage, no matter what the protests and pain expressed by the "learner," they all also at some point expressed doubt and hesitated. When a teacher/subject did hesitate, the experimenter recited a script of replies, starting with "please continue" to the final "you have no choice, you must go on." At that point, if the teacher still refused, the experiment ended. But if the teacher did go all the way to what he believed to be the maximum of 450 volts, the experimenter had him administer it twice more, and then the experiment was ended. As already mentioned, in this version of the experiment, 26 out of 40 teachers went all the way to the maximum.

Milgram and his students, and his colleagues in the psychology department at Yale, had already been astounded at how far subjects would go in an earlier pilot version. After his official grant started, he wrote to the head of social sciences at NSF in September of 1961:

> I once wondered whether in all of the United States a vicious government could find enough moral imbeciles to meet the personnel requirements of a national system of death camps of the sort that were maintained in Germany. I am now beginning to think that the full complement could be recruited in New Haven. A substantial proportion of people do what they are told to do, irrespective of the content of the act, and without pangs of conscience, so long as they perceive that the command comes from a legitimate authority (pg. 100).

Was this experiment for real in the subjects' eyes? Much ink has been spilled over that question. Surveys were conducted that indicate that most subjects in this and later versions thought they really were administering shocks. But by and large, they were alright with what the experiment had put them through, after the "debriefing" and after meeting the team member who had played the "learner" and seeing that he was alright. Other sources, like some case studies of former subjects that Blass describes, suggest that it was a trauma that didn't go away. At the same time, some who were traumatized also praised the experiment for teaching them to stand up to authority.

Was the experiment real to the teacher-subjects *during* its actual performance? As noted above, most thought they were actually administering shocks. Look at some of the YouTube videos for yourself. Milgram, in his first article about the work published in 1963, wrote:

> In a large number of cases the degree of tension reached
> extremes that are rarely seen in sociopsychological labo-
> ratory studies. Subjects were observed to sweat, tremble,
> stutter, bite their lips, groan, and dig their fingernails into
> their flesh. These were characteristic rather than excep-
> tional responses to the experiment. (pg. 122-23)

The explosion of ethical debate that descriptions like this set off
is well described in Blass's book. Remember, this was before Insti-
tutional Review Boards that had to clear human social research
for "protection of human subjects." The controversy followed
Milgram for the rest of his life.

Back to Human Universals

How did this theatrical production of a hypothesis-free and
theory-avoiding BSS study become one of the most important
experiments in history? Blass thinks it

> …has to do with the fact that, in his demonstration of our
> powerful propensity to obey authority, Milgram has iden-
> tified one of the universals of social behavior—one that
> transcends both time and place—and people intuitively
> sense this (pg. 283).

By way of supporting this universal claim, Blass includes an overview of numerous Milgram-like studies done in the U.S. and other
countries. "Remarkably," he writes, "the average obedience rates
were very similar" (pg. 309). A full review of differences by social
category is beyond the scope of this book. On the whole, though,

it sounds as if there just weren't that many. Men and women, for example, came up with more or less the same results in the classic experiment.

This point about universals is the one I expected to make about BSS by looking at Milgram's work. Authority figures have been around forever. It was one of Donald Brown's universals when he wrote about culture as part of being human, as described in the previous chapter.   Cases of individual angst when people are told by an authority to do something against their values and their own interests—it must be a universal dilemma, part of how the human social world works, everywhere. I'll bet that it is a plot point in stories everywhere, "stories" being another universal. What Milgram showed was how powerful an authority could be, more powerful than anyone had imagined. That was the universal that Milgram tested, and the results still stand.

He did develop the obedience studies further. He changed the experiment to require more of a direct personal connection between teacher and learner, and that change meant more teachers quit before the 450-volt maximum. He also designed some experiments that showed that, if you loaded the experiment up with *three* teachers—two of them stooges from the research team, and then those two quit early—the actual subject would almost always follow suit and quit early as well.

Details on this, and on the many other projects Milgram created before and after the obedience studies, are available in Blass's book. In some ways the obedience research was a classic BSS study, but in other ways it wasn't. No theory, no hypothesis, and an experimental setting out of a Hollywood production designer's dream. It wasn't HSR, but HSR leaked into it from several different sources. In Milgram's case, BSS used HSR to get more grounded and real, more "ecologically valid," to resurrect that BSS concept one more time.

Universals were the place I really wanted to land in, to show the power of BSS to investigate and challenge any universal claim. "X is a universal" is a clear proposition that lends itself to a deductive test in the style of John Stuart Mill's joint method. It goes without saying that the deduction doesn't only need to be tested in the laboratory. And the test needs to be run over and over again, everywhere. If it is a universal it will show up over and over again, everywhere. But this kind of work can only deal with universal *fragments*, and fragments are nowhere near the coherent theory that we need of what it is that makes us human.

To move towards such a coherent theory, we have to cycle back to HSR again and look at the universal in its home territory, namely, everyday human social life, to see how it might shape-shift in the context of different human social patterns. Doing something against one's will or one's values because of the request or command of an authority figure—there's a lot more work to do here, and a lot more places to look for problem cases.

Taking Milgram back to the HSR ground would teach us more about how various dimensions of intentionality and lived experience could interact to dress the universal in local color. Even the experience of the experiment—I kept wanting to know more about the individuals who refused among that first all-male sample, and how that refusal developed in the intersubjective space of the actual experiment.

I recently visited a Zapatista village in Southern Mexico. On the wall of one building stood Zapata's famous saying, "It is better to die on your feet than to live on your knees." I wonder what a Zapatista would do in a Milgram experiment run by a white-coated professor? But then I wonder what he would do if the authority figure telling him to keep shocking the learner was a baklava-clad pipe-smoking Subcomandante instead of a professor from Yale?

And if the "learner" was an elite landowner known for his abuse of campesinos? Fill in the blanks for your own authority/learner worst case scenario.

No Researcher Before His Time

Milgram's obedience research had an impact that most human social science only dreams of. It had the sex appeal of a scandal sheet—look what people will do to each other just because they were told to. He broke all sorts of BSS rules. He didn't much care about theory and hypothesis. When a committee from the National Science Foundation visited him, the team leader observed with some displeasure that it was "clear that Dr. Milgram neither has nor plans to have an elaborate a priori theory." (pg. 71). As his biographer Blass summarizes one example of a reviewer's comment on a journal article:

> Foreshadowing a kind of criticism that would dog Milgram for most of his career, Jones faulted him for not having any theory to illuminate his findings, which Jones dismissed as "a kind of triumph of social engineering" (pg. 114).

And after completing the project, Milgram had difficulties getting the results published in professional journals, in spite of—or perhaps because of—the fact that he wrote in a clear jargon-free style.

This is the dark side of the famous "peer review," the idea that colleague evaluation necessarily insures quality. That same "evaluation" can also suppress rather than support innovation. Milgram called the obsession with hypothesis testing, one of the elements a BSS peer reviewer would likely require, a "common fallacy." Writing about his earlier work in Norway and France, he said that:

> At this stage of cross-national research, when even simple, objective descriptions of national groups have not been attained, an experiment is no more in need of an hypothesis than is a thermometer. The utility of a measuring instrument does not depend on the guess we make about its reading (pg. 40).

I smiled when I read that, remembering the words of one of my profs in graduate school, one of the most mathematically sophisticated researchers I've ever known. He talked about the incredible (he meant unbelievably stupid) notion of science as only the testing of hypotheses.

Milgram was a BSS maverick with HSR tendencies. He paid for his peculiarities. An ethics controversy broke out that continued for the rest of his career. The irony is, he had worried about ethics, in this project and in his earlier dissertation research, long before it was required. Harvard denied him a permanent position and Blass writes that he had trouble with other job offers because the faculty was uncomfortable with his experiment. The academic routines of publishing and grant-getting became more difficult for him as time went on. The American Psychological Association never did give him its award for Distinguished Scientific Contributions. On the other hand, there was massive uptake of his work in the popular media, in the arts, in business and the military, in legal scholarship and practice, and of course in human social science of all kinds. But the response of his academic discipline was more punitive than enthusiastic. He told us humans things we didn't want to know about ourselves and he did it in a way that caused colleagues to squirm at ethical questions over how he forced the story out.

At the same time, Milgram, and many others, saw his

obedience experiments as helping understand a historic event that was on everyone's mind in the 1950s, as it still is today, the mass murder of Jews by the Nazis in World War II. Milgram was Jewish. Blass quotes him:

> [My] laboratory paradigm . . . gave scientific expression to a more general concern about authority, a concern forced upon members of my generation, in particular upon Jews such as myself, by the atrocities of World War II. . . . The impact of the Holocaust on my own psyche energized my interest in obedience and shaped the particular form in which it was examined (pg. 62).

Blass notes that Milgram decided to do the obedience experiments at about the same time as Adolf Eichmann was apprehended in Argentina and taken to Israel to stand trial.

Milgram's work gains significance with his biographical and historical situation. He is a researcher, but he is also a person with his own contexts and meanings, existing in a historical time. This observation doesn't discredit the research as "unscientific." It enriches the audience's—that is, our—understanding of the work and makes its results even more terrifying and profound than they otherwise would have been.

The link to the Holocaust opens up discussion of a profound HSR-like critique. The obedience work provided the "scientific underpinnings," as Blass put it, for Hannah Arendt's famous concept of the "banality of evil." She argued that the trial of Eichmann in Jerusalem didn't reveal the monster that the Israeli prosecution wanted to show the world. Instead, he came across as a dull bureaucrat who, in fact, really did see himself as "just following orders." Milgram's experiment showed much the same thing, how people would "just follow orders," though he made it very clear that "explaining" did not mean "excusing."

Arendt's—and Milgram's—conclusions about the Holocaust were challenged by several people and by additional sources of information from the lived experience of World War II. Stories were told about sadism and torture and murder. The biggest critic of Arendt turned out to be Arendt herself when she wrote about the later trial of twenty-two SS guards from Auschwitz in the mid 1960s. As Blass summarized it:

> ...there was another face to the Holocaust besides that of the dutiful bureaucrat, and she stated that the Frankfurt trial "in many respects reads like a much-needed supplement to the Jerusalem trial." So, while her phrase "banality of evil" has been adopted by some to describe the essential nature of Nazi destructiveness, it would seem that Arendt herself recognized a broader truth (pg. 276).

Even as powerful and grounded and close to lived experience as Milgram's experiment was, it still drew boundaries around the phenomenon of interest that restricted its connection to the real human social world. What Milgram found was true to life, in part, but life had also included those who enthusiastically acted with a viciousness and hatred that went well beyond doing what an authority figure requested under duress.

In the end I know on a personal level that there's more HSR work to do here. I lived through the Waldheim scandal in Austria in the 1980s, when that famous Austrian figure's World War II record turned out to be more complicated than his public version of it. I remember him saying, repeatedly, "I only did my duty." By then I'd learned that, in German, "duty" or "Pflicht" conveys a more powerful personal responsibility to authority than "duty" does in English.

I wondered how Milgram's experiment might have gone if the "learner" was of a social category that the teacher hated. I know it's a gruesome thought, but what if we ran a Milgram experiment today with two social types with deep emotional dislike of each other based on social identities of race or class or gender or nationality or religion? You see what I mean? That would be the experiment to test what Arendt learned in her second experience, the Frankfurt trials of the sadistic camp guards. In the context of what kind of pattern might hesitation to throw the switch turn into enthusiasm for the job?

In the end, I have to admit that my use of Milgram's work is as self-referential as was Milgram's use of it for himself, only in a different mix of biography and history. My years of involvement in Austria, starting as a high-school exchange student and continuing through several visits, some long term, have tangled me up with Austrians of my generation, all of us born right around the end of World War II and stuck for life dealing with Nazi history on a deeply personal level. It's much too complicated a story to tell here. Some of it is in my book *Language Shock*. I've been—and continue to be—as preoccupied with the Nazi past as they are, because "I" became part "they" over the years. Hitler, as many readers will know, was Austrian, and Eichmann, though born in Germany, grew up in the same Austrian province as Hitler did, the same province where I lived as an American exchange student when I first heard about "the war" from an Austrian first person point of view.

Stories of both collaboration and resistance are real, stories of "just following orders," or of living in fear, of heroic resistance, of enthusiasm for the Reich. The Nazi ghosts remain a heavy presence in everyday life among my Austrian age group. It's more complex—in both the ordinary sense of "complicated" and the technical sense of "complexity"—than simple presence or absence of an authority giving an order that contradicts values that you, the subject, hold dear. Milgram helps understand *some* of what happened during World War II in universal human terms, but there's a lot more to it than what he showed in the experiment. I haven't done much official research on the topic, but I've walked a lot of that ground for decades.

Still, a link between researcher biography and history and an actual project—the "self reference" theme writ large—it doesn't diminish the importance of the obedience experiment. In fact, it adds to it. It certainly doesn't make it "unscientific." I admire Milgram for showing that "it could have happened here," where "here" means anywhere in the human social world. Sometimes, in my own private thoughts, I think that was what drove him. He wanted to show America that brutal treatment of "the other" wasn't a Nazi monopoly, something he probably already knew from his own lived experience.

In Whose Interests?

Milgram shows how self-reference, the fact that a scientist works in a historical context that shapes research, does not convert into "anti-science" at all. His story also casts some shadows on the notion of academic freedom. Milgram crafted his science in large part in a struggle *against* his academic context, not with its support. Some of that struggle centered on his HSR tendencies in a BSS world, something the original SocRel program at Harvard was meant to encourage.

Human social science is all too human, and that simple truth has to be part of its epistemology rather than being swept under the carpet and consigned to the late night barroom conversation at the annual conference. I'd like to take that premise and expand it as a conclusion for this book, because it's not just self-reference around a particular project, as the obedience research illustrates. It also fits into the topic of self-reference in terms of power and money and the rules of the game that shape the space of a research project and therefore limit the possible paths it can take.

This bigger picture leads to all kinds of general questions. Like who in their right mind pays for human social science research and why would they ever do that? And why does some researcher want to do a particular research project in the first place? And why in the world would any sane person be a research subject? And who pays attention to anything human social science does and why do they do that?

Questions like these have to be folded into an epistemology as well. Many traditional BSS types view them as yet another shovelful of "anti-science," as more steps down the path to hell paved with historical, cultural and moral relativity. They are not that at all. On the contrary, a failure to ask them is the height of naiveté. Much of what we learn in a specific project—BSS or HSR or any science for that matter—emerges out of a moment of history, out of a convergence of power and money to which science responds if it seeks financial support and an audience for its work.

Science in the substance abuse field is alive with the sound of this naiveté. After decades as a researcher and program and policy consultant, I could tell stories for the rest of the new millennium. Some of them are in the book *Dope Double Agent* that I've mentioned before. I used to joke that I was grateful that the Vietnam War forced me to work in the U.S. drug field at a time—1968—when the "War on Drugs" was just rearing its ugly head. It taught me, at the tender age of twenty-two, immediately and with massive personal impact, that the concept of "objective research" on illegal drugs was a worse hallucination than a trip brought on by an overdose of really bad LSD.

For instance, funding agencies, with almost no exceptions, only supported human social science projects that asked, "What is *wrong* with *abuse* of illegal drug X?" It's a fair question, except that "abuse" was seldom defined in any clear way, certainly in no way that approached the standards of an adequate epidemiological "case record," as they call it. Besides, "abuse" is not exactly a value-free term. Any proposal that even hinted at the question, "What is *right* with *use* of illegal drug X?" was tossed out, even though that, too, was and is a fair question.

War on Drugs politics, with funding agencies falling into line right behind their political budget controllers, dictated that even one use of an illegal drug counted as abuse and that not even that one use could ever be considered a positive thing. Many readers will know better from their own lived experience. So did a fair number of the political controllers who in those days prayed that no journalist would ever ask what in Washington in the 1980s they called the "M" question—"Have you ever smoked marijuana?" And even if a reader of this book is a drug virgin, surely he will agree that from a scientific point of view, a question about positive effects is not only reasonable. It is an important scientific one if the point is to understand attraction to a chemical, illegal or legal, as well as possible dependency on it.

And why, one might also ask, did so many researchers shift their interests to this new substance abuse field? It barely existed in the mid-1960s. No sooner did President Nixon institutionalize the drug war by littering the Washington landscape with new agencies and budgets than "drug research" became popular. Lucky me, I stumbled in at the right time, though I stumbled in because it offered me an escape from my own personal contradictory devils. "Serving my country," sounded right; the Vietnam War was insane. I did take advantage of the new drug money as time went on, though. Let he who is without guilt first get stoned, or however the drug version of that biblical saying would go.

I watched the drug field explode around me. There was, all of a sudden, gold in them thar' dope-riddled hills, and getting a grant earned a field promotion in the academic wars as well. On the other hand, I also learned that among many academics, dope money was a sign of ill breeding. "Drugs, I mean, what were you thinking, it's so *political*." No scholar should ever deal with such complicated messy dirty things. Philosopher-kings were better off in Plato's cave. The shadows were good enough.

And why were drug-dependent people bothering to answer the questions that the new flock of researchers posed? Most research subjects were poor people who were seeking help in government institutions, the same government that had already decided what "drug abuse" was. Those poor people had to answer questions to get in and stay in, and the institutions had to ask those questions and produce statistics as a condition of funding. In another frequent scenario, subjects were poor and needed cash, and research grants paid them to be a subject, a little (from the researcher point of view) and a lot (from their point of view). In the streets of Baltimore in the early 2000s, payments for research participation in any area were called "study money." The U.S. drug field was built on the backs of poor people who needed free treatment or a little cash.

I've gone on and on about all this in other places. The drug field is easy to parody, because it is so overloaded with emotional and political freight. I quit in exhaustion in the mid-2000s. I'm only mentioning a few highlights now to show, once again, that the BSS claim of objectivity is naïve, that any human social science is by definition intersubjective. The only news here is that, in this final section of the book, I'm adding that "intersubjective" also means a broad and deep historical context in which research is proposed, funded and received in an equally broad and deep network of human interests. There are many "subjects" involved in the bigger picture—communities, funders, audiences, policy makers, voters, and many more in in governments and civil society and the markets.

We can replace "objectivity" with a more useful question, though, one that gets at the credibility problem in a more suitable way. Why should we believe the results of human social research? Instead of a call for an objectivity that is delusional when human subjects research others, we can ask about the *interests* of subjects involved in the research, and then expand out from there into the interests of those who supported the research and those who used it after it was done.

Exactly Who and Why

Jürgen Habermas developed a general framework for thinking about all this. It centered on the concept of "knowledge and human interests," a phrase that is an academic cliché in his native German, "Erkentnisinteresse." "Interest" means a desire that a research project happen at all, and then perhaps a desire that it end in a particular way, together with the power on the part of those interests to influence the process that brings the research results about by paying for it, say, or distributing it, or implementing it.

I heard that classic German word-made-out-of-words all the time in conversations during visits to the University of Vienna. It means, roughly translated, "Who has a stake in this knowledge and why do they care?" Out of Habermas' concept spills a list of questions to ask of any human social science project, or any project at all for that matter, questions that get at the sorts of problems that "objectivity" is supposed to handle but doesn't. The questions help evaluate an "intersubjective" science when it is being examined for its credibility.

Such questions that a person might ask include: What interests did the project serve and why were those interests there in the first place? Who paid for the project? Why did they think it was worth paying for? What problem did those with the money have that they hoped the research would solve? Why did the researchers take the job? What kinds of limits were imposed on what they could do? Why did research subjects allow the research to happen at all? For love? For money? Because they had no other choice? What was in it for them? What did they think of it when it was done? Or did anyone even care? And who was the audience for the final report, or the film, or the museum exhibit? What kind of effect on that audience did the funders want the project to have? What effect did it in fact have in the end?

Habermas is the prominent living heir to the famous "Frankfurt School." Among the more interesting things it argued was how the tradition of natural science made it easy to adapt human social science to the political status quo, a useful skill if a researcher depends on the state or any other group with ideological goals for funds.

Here's how that works: Traditional social science starts with a theory from which a hypothesis is derived. Where do theories come from? Humans make them up. They describe human social worlds and explain why they are as they are. What theories tend to get funded for research by a government? Theories that define perceived problems and offer hypotheses that fit their way of thinking about the world. The problem that worried the Frankfurt School was, once a theory is in play, traditional scientific control takes over and closes the doors to complicating and possibly contradictory information from the world of human subjects. A researcher can do great research with the most ideologically biased of hypotheses. The only possible criticism is that a hypothesis is not supported. So far so good, but then what kind of alternative theory is there? None that ventures outside the same politics that supported the first one. That was, still is for the most part, the story of what happened in the U.S. drug field, as described in the previous section. They started in an ideological box and didn't work their way out of it for decades. Much more to say here and—I'm glad to report—a couple of recent events, as of 2013, that show retreat from the War on Drugs front.

But then if we abandon old-fashioned notions of objectivity in the human social science realm—as I have several times now—how do we answer the justifiable and important question to ask of any argument, research-based or otherwise. *Why should I believe this?* The first answer was offered in Chapter Four of this book. It featured Toulmin's argumentation diagram, more flexible and fluid than a traditional laboratory, but still carrying the responsibility to make a case based on evidence, logic, and falsification with a transparency that allows critical evaluation. Habermas layers in some additional questions that go beyond a Toulmin diagram. What human interests were in play around a particular project, starting with who supported it, who did it, who let it be done to them, and who used it for what ends?

There is a major difference between the two kinds of

evaluations. In the case of Toulmin, we can look and say, this case was well made, or that case lacks evidence, or logic, or falsification. But with Habermas' human interests, the evaluation is different. It's not a "yes" or "no" question. Interests are *always* there. It's never a question of whether they were there or were not. They are *part of* the science, always, not better or worse ways of doing it. The question isn't, "Are interests influencing the project?" The question is, "Is it clear what those interests are and how they shaped the space within which a project emerged and the path that it eventually took?"

Interests aren't necessarily a bad thing of course. They can't be, because they are always present and good science—human social or otherwise—is in fact done in a context that includes them. The fact that Milgram shaped his study in part under the influence of post-war questions about the Holocaust doesn't make it less credible or useful. In fact, the larger historical context gives it more significance than it otherwise might have had. The fact that an outpatient chemo clinic wanted to improve care for their patients—a case I described in the first chapter of this book— that's a good thing by anyone's values. The fact that—during the madness of the "war on drugs"—a nonprofit now called the Drug Policy Alliance used some human social research to criticize that policy in ways that are finally now coming to fruition is, for me, like an oxygen bar after decades of holding my breath.

A grand illusion, to borrow another movie title, is the blinders put on science and its public in the name of "objectivity." It bypasses the critical importance of looking at the multiple human interests involved in a project, interests that partly explain project outcomes, including outcomes that are *absent* because any project that might have led to them would never have been supported. This is a simple fact, and it can't be said enough. Human social science projects in particular—projects more generally than that—are always in part a function of global, national, organizational, and individual interests that want to see them happen. Or that *don't* want them to happen, as the case may be. Science without human interests is impossible as long as the actors involved in it are human as well.

HSR makes the self-reference even more visible. Those who write the rules and provide the resources for projects have a vested interest in their *own* intentionality and lived experience, what the human social science types would call their ideology, what I think of as naïve realism with political and economic teeth. HSR features a call for uncontrolled evidence from the human social worlds of subjects and takes it seriously as part of the data. That doesn't always go over so well when it contradicts or undermines the image of subjects and self held by those who control the power and the money who called for the research in the first place. The results, at a bare minimum, can make the human social world more complicated, contradictory and problematic than they ever wanted to know.

My experience is, such results can go either way. Sometimes a funder/authority is happy to learn about differences, including differences in views of themselves, but other times they want me—and the subjects—to go away. There are many stories in the literature of applied human social science to draw on here, another book to write one day. In the end, though, human social science has to be about how the human social world works, not about how the powers-that-be would like to believe it does. That attitude echoes the anti-authoritarian stance that started modern science on its centuries-long history. Founders like Bacon and Galileo said, you know, maybe Aristotle and the Bible didn't have this right after all. That commitment to cases based on evidence, logic and falsification can cause a human social scientist as much trouble as the Inquisition caused Galileo. Milgram wasn't put under house arrest like Galileo was, but, the way Blass tells it, he paid for his maverick work.

HSR and BSS both require human social relationships in order to happen at all. They are *intersubjective* sciences. They require social relationships with those who support the science, those who do it, those who serve as subjects of it, and those who consume it. Human social science—science in general—is also a human social world. In order to make any of these relationships function, never mind all of them at once, there is pressure to *adapt*, to shape a project to make sense to the human actors who support it, do it, participate in it, and consume it.

The difficult judgment call for the researcher is this: To some extent he or she *should* translate his or her own framework and jointly build a framework for communication with subjects of all those different types. That was the point of the previous chapter about the intersubjective space of the research. The bedrock of intersubjective research isn't to preach or to lecture, but rather to learn and to communicate the results, though not at the price of abandoning the core principles of the science. The pressure always exists to achieve a balance, and a researcher always has to make the call of how much and in what way to handle it.

This fact has to be part of the science, not to mention a central part of training for human social researchers. How to navigate this ambiguous territory with professional integrity and product quality is a neglected topic, a neglect understandable in light of academic traditions where one could assume that whatever the dissertation committee or disciplinary peers would like was the right thing to do. That isolation is no longer possible. In my view, taking human social research out into the world makes it more difficult, more interesting, more intellectually challenging, and of higher moral value than it ever has been. I would say that, since that's what I started doing fifteen years ago. But my motives are more than just cognitive dissonance.

The Jewish Nun

I'd like to end with a story that I tried to tell in several different places in the book. It didn't really fit in any earlier sections because it is about too many of them all at once. The story is about Edith Stein and her work on empathy. She brings Brentano and Dilthey closer to how one human in contact with another can see the surprising "Q" and create the abducted "P" in the lived experience of a research project. She also makes it clear that this abstract goal actually involves translation across different meanings and contexts. She describes a natural human ability that makes human social science possible at all, an ability that brings together researcher self-reference, an intersubjective encounter, and the goal of building a rational reconstruction to make sense of the differences. Her work and my discovery of it are full of self-reference—both mine and hers—that shows how research takes its shape in webs of broader political interests.

Besides, she represents a refreshing change. Until now, the main sources I have relied on have mostly been the proverbial dead white guys, mostly Austrians or Germans, or people influenced by them. They are among the major intellectual beacons of HSR that I grew up with, and as a German speaker who has worked often in Austria—though very rusty at the language now—they were part of the ocean I swam in for decades. Their influence made me the epistemological train wreck I am today.

It's 2013 as I finish writing this book. The question came to mind as I worked on it, as it should now, "Where are the women and people of color who were part of the early HSR story?" Nowadays, of course, the demographics of the various fields that use HSR are as diverse as the world is. If I had to make a bet, I'd guess that the ranks of the professionals are majority female and well populated with social categories from the entire global menu. Surely somebody besides old white guys had something to say about HSR in its formative years?

Here's what drove the question. James Watson published a book in 1968, *The Double Helix*, about the discovery of DNA, usually attributed to him and Francis Crick. It stirred up a lot of negative press from his science colleagues, because he wrote about the human social world of the scientists who created the double helix model, now called the genome. The book was a scandal when it appeared. It included the scientists in the science and revealed the "dark underbelly of the laboratory." Ambition, unseemly passions, gossip—how dare he!

Brenda Maddox, much later in 2003, wrote a book about a woman named Rosalind Franklin, the scientist who produced the images that suggested and then supported Watson and Crick's famous double helix model. The book was subtitled "The Dark Lady of DNA." Franklin was quoted as calling Watson's book "Jim's novel." "Jim" Watson's description of the DNA story was fatheaded nonsense as far as she was concerned.

Franklin's version of the DNA story, and her biography, are complicated. She was marginalized, dumped, and left out of the Nobel Prize. She was also, in the tradition of men dealing with women who don't smile and admire everything they say, called "difficult." And for all I know, she might really have been a pain to deal with. Gender doesn't predict presence or absence of that characteristic, not in my lived experience. But one thing has always been clear. She was a major contributor and she was left out of the story of DNA and the awards and recognition that came with it.

Looking back from present times, the main theme of Franklin's story is not a surprise. It has been shown, over and over again, how the structures in which we live and work foreground some voices and hide others. The voices that are hidden are usually non-male or non-European ancestry or both. It's a cliché now because its truth has become so obvious, case after case. The white male working class and poor worlds that I know from my youth and from my own research, whose voices are also frequently hidden, don't always get equal time in this argument because they're male and white, but that's a complaint for another day. Read Arthur Miller's 1949 play *The Death of a Salesman* sometime for an example of what I mean. That timeless play is running yet again on Broadway in 2012.

Thinking of Franklin's story, I kept wondering as I worked on *The Lively Science*, where is the "dark lady" of 19th century HSR?

Edith Stein (1891-1942) was a student of Husserl, who in turn was a student of Brentano. She studied with Husserl during the mid-1920s and then became a colleague in the field of phenomenology. A daughter of a large Jewish family in Breslau, then a part of the German empire, she became an atheist, then converted to Christianity, then became a Catholic nun in 1934. Husserl refused to recommend her for a university position in spite of her professional qualifications. She taught at a Catholic girl's school and translated Aquinas, then finally obtained a university position in 1932. In 1933, Nazi anti-Semitic laws were enacted and she was forced to resign. She fled to the Netherlands but was arrested there in 1942 after the German occupation of that country. She was sent to the concentration camp in Auschwitz and killed because of her Jewish ancestry. In 1990, she was canonized by the Catholic Church as Saint Teresa Benedicta of the Cross. B'nai Brith complained.

This is a horrible, not to mention bizarre, story. But Stein's philosophical work, now being rediscovered, was extraordinary. In her phenomenological days, Stein took the Brentano and Husserl philosophical stream and aimed it at a problem in their work, the same one that concerns this book, namely, how can different intentionalities and lived experiences be connected to understand another person's point of view in terms of one's own? The founders of phenomenology centered on the self, the individual, the single human agent. Humans could "bracket" experience and think their way into what Husserl called an "epoché," a transcendental universal state where the true nature of the phenomenon would become apparent. The problem for Stein and for HSR? It's all done in the privacy of the bracketer's own mind.

Stein reworked this problem so that HSR could keep one's self in the picture but also include the "other." She made phenomenology *intersubjective*. Brentano, remember, switched psychology from a third to a first person perspective, where the "first person" was the scientist looking at his or her own mental phenomena. Stein shifted it again, to a third person perspective on a different first person, where the third person was the scientist, and the first person was the research subject. The scientist's goal turned into how to learn something about their *joint* first person perspective, *first person plural*.

Stein went right to the heart of the intersubjective problem. She made the "my mind" of Brentano into a "me and your mind in contact" to forge a connection that showed how understanding across different intentionalities and lived experiences was possible. HSR became a *social* act that included researcher and subject both.

The key concept in her work was *empathy*, "Einfühlung" in German. The term suggests "feeling into" someone else. Like her teachers, and like those who followed in the Brentano tradition, her writing is difficult. One web site about Stein seemed particularly clear to me, so I'm going to quote from it.

> According to Stein, empathy is defined as "acts in which foreign experience is comprehended." She also describes empathy as "how human beings comprehend the psychic life of their fellows." Let me restate in today's terminology: Stein's empathy is an unflinching encounter with alterity (otherness). For an encounter to be empathy, Stein says, we must refuse to reduce the "other" to the horizon of the same.

In other words, no naïve realism. And later:

> How, then, can a human person have a truly empathic encounter? The answer lies in de-centering the self through a transcendent exercise of the free will. Stein says: "we lock ourselves into the prison of our individuality" when "we take the self as the standard." To avoid assimilation and suppression when encountering another, the human person has to stop using his/her own self as the standard of reality. Stein describes a process of empathy whose core is making the other person subject and not object.

Stein's analysis of empathy, and her later writing that spun out its consequences for social life and collective action, foreshadow much of what would become foundational HSR work in contemporary times. Consider George Herbert Mead, another major figure neglected in this book. He studied in Germany—by now we could have guessed—was active in social and political causes, and developed the American pragmatics tradition that had started with the same Peirce who created abductive logic. Mead inspired an HSR wing pasted onto a very large BSS sociology bird, called *symbolic interactionism*, and, like Festinger's cognitive dissonance, it spawned multitudes. He showed how even things we consider the private property of individuals—mind and self—were products of social life. Mead could have been Stein's student. I'd take a bet that he at least studied her work.

Stein brought phenomenology, one legacy of Franz Brentano, down to the ground of actual encounters *between* humans rather than something an individual human discovers in a personal transcendental moment. For purposes of this book, it is easy to see her argument in terms of the Toulmin diagram that HSR research needs to build. A person does something. Another person, in this case a researcher, wonders what it is and why it was done. That second person builds up an "as if" abduction to describe and explain the differences. Based on what? Based on empathy, on the common ground of human lived experience and intentionality. But one can't use oneself as the only "standard of reality," as Stein described her version of naïve realism. A connection must be worked out, a translation, an encounter with the "foreign." The rational reconstruction *includes* the beliefs, desires and purposes of *both* research subjects and the researcher. It is a blend based on a translation.

Empathy is central. Empathy foregrounds how researcher and subject both have to be included in the science for a rational reconstruction to be built at all, and rational reconstruction in a Toulmin-like framework is the starting point for HSR science. Any Toulmin-like case that is made as a result will include at least two human intentionalities. The scientist's voice inevitably dominates the final scientific report, but the case that she makes will include the voices and actions of subjects as well. The science is *intersubjective*—that critical word again—based on what happens *between* subjects, neither objective nor subjective in any simple way. That intersubjective space, that working out of a translation, is the foundation of human social science, and empathy makes it possible.

As an altar boy veteran, I can't get the thought out of my mind, meant with the highest respect, "Hochachtung" the Germans would say, Saint Teresa Benedicta, pray for us.

The End

Conclusions have always been a problem for me. A book is its own conclusion. Writing a summary at the end makes some sense, but I always figure that if the reader hasn't gotten the main theme by then, either I've failed in the writing or they've failed in the reading or the chemistry just didn't work, like a bad blind date.

The main point of *The Lively Science* is that human social science took a fork in the road a couple of hundred years ago and it went in the wrong direction. It took the "follow the model of natural science" turnoff. It was wrong because humans and their groups have characteristics—intentionality and lived experience—that the natural sciences had no experience with, except in the privacy of their own home.

The "remodeling" of human social science that this book promised was about taking those characteristics seriously and rebuilding a way of thinking about evidence, logic and falsification that placed them squarely in the center of the science. I'm sure I skidded off the trail here and there and no doubt got some things wrong that I'll hear about from colleagues. But if that core message didn't come through, then one of us, dear reader, messed up, or else we just weren't meant to be in a writer/reader relationship.

Why did I bother? Many others have tried to reach a general audience with this message. In anthropology the late Clifford Geertz was probably the most prominent public intellectual carrying the HSR gospel to the North American world. But then I know from experience that his words didn't work, more often than not. Consider his famous concept of "thick description," a concept imported and tossed around in many areas of the real world. I've heard it used over and over again in more work contexts than I can remember. But most everyone heard "thick" as "a lot of material," so a thick description contains more than you ever wanted to know about what is being described. Like a four hour video of a one-day family vacation.

Fine, but that's not what he meant. "Thick" meant the many levels of meaning and context that interact with each other when a particular social moment is interpreted. An eye-wink can modify a tone of voice which can modify the literal content of what was said which can be inappropriate to the context but the eye-wink tells you it's a joke.

> "Oh I love fast food," said Julia Child with an enthusiastic tone of voice, winking at her audience at the gourmet cooking convention.

"Thick" was about how human social science was different because of what humans could do with meaning and context, not about how it was a good thing to mindlessly add shovelfuls of detail of whatever it was one was describing. So if the great Geertz didn't get the message across to a general audience—and he was great—then maybe a try from the trenches couldn't do any harm and might even help.

Well, "trenches" is a little dramatic. My life has been a lot more comfortable than that. I usually have a warm bed to sleep in and a pistol was only pointed at my head once. What I mean, as I've mentioned several times in this book, is that a lot of what I write here comes from experiences working with non-academics in organizations, not from teaching in an academic setting or doing traditional human social science research, though I've done those things as well.

People I dealt with were smart, and they were risk-takers, or else I wouldn't have been asked to work on things with them. They had been trained into a mentality that wanted to see "the numbers" or "hard data" that was "objective," or the latest "model" generated by some sexy new "software." Their problem was, the "numbers" weren't solving their problem, or even defining it in a way that made sense. Readers who know the organizational literature will recognize that calling for an alternative to "the numbers" is not news. It starts as far back as foundational writings by Peter Drucker, though those same readers will also know that the "show me the numbers" mindset still dominates day-to-day management of organizations of all types.

The risk-taking part meant that it wasn't normal to seek out someone like me to help figure out how to build knowledge in a different way that changed the view of a problem and the people involved in it. Since the risk-takers had no intention of becoming organizational kamikazes, though, they wanted to understand what this different thing I did was, how it worked, and why they should believe its results. They asked good questions, and kept asking them as time went on.

An academic lecture loaded with footnotes and jargon and

dense textual powerpoints that only a dissertation committee could love wasn't the answer they sought. They wanted an intelligible conversation that mixed theory and practice and real world examples into a single blend, very much the kind of attitude that motivated Stephen Toulmin to develop his model of making a case. They were after a "blurred genre," to use another Geertz concept, neither academic diatribe nor puff piece nor scandal sheet, just something clear and credible and useful.

With *The Lively Science* I wanted to take dozens of those conversations and organize them into a book. Besides, inside the academic world the problem of how to think about HSR in general is of increasing interest as well. As I was revising the book for the eighth or ninth million time, I attended a public lecture by Robert May, partly because I'd never heard a genuine Baron speak before. I expected upper, upper dialect and witty but demeaning references to Americans, like the characters on the TV show MI5 make all the time. No such thing, he was a pretty nice guy, maybe a slumming Baron, I don't know. I really went to hear him because for me he's a nonlinear dynamic hero, one of the founders who created ecological models based on complexity science.

Here's what happened. In response to a question after the talk, he mused that really the problem with issues of climate change was a problem on human social science grounds. The physics and the chemistry were simple, he said. But, he added, we don't know how to get the human social science part right. The audience was mostly natural science, so there was a brief and sympathetic flurry of "why can't they get it right?" comments. Well, said May, there are some promising signs recently and, without elaboration, he moved on with relief to the next question.

I went home and went back to work. May and his audience were the perfect example of how people, usually with the best of intentions, think the way to make human social science better is to make it more like natural science. They mean well, most of them, but natural science just doesn't get intentionality and lived experience. They want to, but they also want the science to be just like them. Mainstream BSS human social science, the so-called "received view," by and large agrees. They have to, because historically natural science was enshrined as the gold standard epistemology to aspire to if any claim of science was to be made at all. Not to mention if a project was to be funded and its results were to be believed.

Why didn't the kind of human social science described in this book, HSR, take off as well? It did in more modest and scattered ways, the more so the closer we get to the present. It's ancestral home in the U.S. for most of the 20th century was a duplex, anthropology and sociology. Anthropology, with its early focus on "traditional" or "primitive" society didn't have much of a choice, because no one really knew much about "the natives" until after they arrived. The scare quotes only mean to show how out of date those old concepts are. And, no surprise in retrospect, the field became famous for not having any methods at all. Sociology developed a subfield, mostly at the University of Chicago, based on Max Weber's goal of finding the abstract notion of "society" in the details of everyday life. That, too, required learning about that life as part of the research and the final report. Since sociology had more of a tradition of self-conscious diatribes about methodology, they talked more about what they did in general. But it still looked pretty touchy-feely compared to quantitative surveys and experimental results.

I'm not quite sure how and why things changed so dramatically. It was partly the era of the 1960s when so many things changed, including pretty much every field in the natural sciences. I'll spare us all a speculative rant that could go on for another book. In human social research, certainly the appearance of *The Discovery of Grounded Theory* by Barney Glaser and Anselm Strauss in 1967 was a key event. In my view it marks a turning point for what became the growth of "qualitative" research." I've criticized that concept a few times in this book and won't repeat it here. But in the end, there is no question: The "qualitative" concept made the idea of an alternative human social science much more widespread than it ever had been before. At the same time, again based on my experience, history fought back such that the old time received view started to assimilate qualitative to its epistemology. Propositional data? Fine, but get it into the laboratory and count its frequency.

More recently, though, I've seen serious HSR grow into fields where I never would have expected it when I first enrolled in an introductory anthropology course in 1964. For example, there is an academic field that some readers may never have heard of, "Speech Communication," with roots in the old idea of teaching rhetoric as part of higher education. An innovative researcher who is now a senior figure, Gerry Philipsen, learned about linguistic anthropologist Dell Hymes' concept of "ethnography of communication" and wrote a book in 1975 called *Speaking Like a Man in Teamsterville*. His work spawned multitudes. That branch of Speech Com, as they call it, held a conference in Portland, around the early/mid 1990s. I thought of the event as "speech communication invites linguistic anthropology for a conversation." It was a great gathering of like-minded people and from that point on I enjoyed the field as a place loaded with HSR colleagues.

More of a shock was a blurb I came across on the Internet a few years ago announcing a summer institute in qualitative research, hosted by the political science department at Arizona State University. I even emailed them just because I had to express my astonishment. They had the good sense not to reply. Apparently the institute had been going since the early 2000s. Political science? Good lord. Who put LSD in John Stuart Mill's office water cooler?

Last year a faculty member in political science, Peregrine Schwartz-Shea heard about a talk I gave and told her colleague Dvora Yanow about it as well. The two of them had just finished their book, *Interpretive Research Design: Concepts and Processes.* They were kind enough to look at an earlier draft of this book. From emails it is obvious that we're on the same wavelength, and that the amount of HSR work in political science in recent years is an entire new field that I need to explore. As a general cover term for HSR, I like their use of "interpretive." It connotes an activity rather than a kind of data like "qualitative" does. And it echoes the later Dilthey, mentioned in passing in Chapter Three, when he moved more and more towards translation and interpretation under the classic Greek name of "hermeneutics."

Those are only two examples of what I see going on around me lately. There are many more. I could tell another story about the qualitative research in management conferences that my colleague Anne Cunliffe runs at the University of New Mexico Business School every other year. Or about my former Baltimore colleagues James Peterson, now a professor in public health, and Heather Reisinger, now running a Veterans Administration research unit, or my colleague Ken Anderson, who runs an HSR group at Intel. And I'm just getting started. So whatever this HSR business is, it is clearly in the ascendancy in several different ways in several different places, both town and gown.

It all makes me wonder if this book was really necessary. My HSR colleagues, especially old-timers like me, would say, "Why bother saying all that again?" I would answer that I *still* hear, from old colleagues and from young researchers alike, on projects and at conferences and via email, that "It's like the last thirty years, never mind the last couple of hundred, never happened." Most of the world still thinks of BSS as the only possible kind of human social science. Most of the world still doesn't get that a different kind of human social science is available, namely HSR, and that it makes more sense to use it if the goal is to describe and explain human social life as humans live it.

And still, the people I worked with on projects were squeamish about letting BSS go. Their subconscious minds held a prejudice born of two hundred years of history: *Not-BSS implied not-science implied not-credible information that no one in their right mind would base a decision on and risk their career for.* I sometimes felt that I'd been hired more as an epistemological therapist to help them work through their anxiety. Deep down they just didn't believe there was life after experimental design, even though they called me in because they knew from experience that it and their problem were miles apart. It was a pleasure to convince them that there was a systematic and transparent alternative.

It looks to me like a—I hate to use the cliché but it seems right here—"paradigm shift" is underway in how we think about human social science in general, and HSR in particular. I'm describing the kind of situation that Thomas Kuhn reported in his classic book, *The Structure of a Scientific Revolution*. It appears to be a time when an alternative human social science that has been waiting in the wings for two centuries has enough momentum and a critical number of practitioners and consumers to develop and apply to human social problems that traditional BSS approaches have failed to solve.

Whether they will do any better remains to be seen. There is evidence so far to place the bet either way. My personal call at the moment, as a researcher with experience in both academic and applied worlds: HSR does work better, on the ground, in problem-oriented research, and people near the problem tend to agree, if they get past how it "doesn't look like science." But the web of interests around a project, more often than not, blocks implementation of the results because it means the hierarchy—scientific or organizational—loses some of its control. As the historian of business Alfred Chandler is famous for saying, structure follows strategy. HSR is good at coming up with new strategies, but the top of the hierarchy usually doesn't want to change the structure. That tentative conclusion calls for another book on implementation.

So, in conclusion, finally, I'm done with this book. I'll probably revise it one of these days. I doubt it'll ever be made into a movie. With time, though, I'll learn to say the things that are in it better. If you, dear reader, have any advice I'd be glad to hear it. Email thelivelyscience@gmail.com if you'd like to let me know.

As they say in New Mexico at the end of a conversation—bueno, bye.

CHAPTER NOTES

Chapter One

The implosion of the "science" concept in anthropology in 2010 received a fair amount of publicity. For example, Nicholas Wade wrote an article in the Science section of the *New York Times* on December 9, 2010, titled "Anthropology a Science? Statement Deepens a Rift." The quote from the Republican leadership comes from a letter to President Obama co-authored by John Boehner and Eric Cantor called "Proposal to Reduce the Deficit and Achieve Savings for American Taxpayers." You can find it on Boehner's web page at www.johnboehner.house.gov.

Most of the social science jokes mentioned in the introductory chapter are well known, or legendary, like Harry Truman's frustration with economists. Should a reader be curious, though, August Comte is worth more work, foundational figure as he was. Michel Bourdeau's entry in the online Stanford Encyclopedia of Philosophy is a good place to start, http://plato.stanford.edu/archives/sum2011/entries/comte.

The famous "theorem" of W.I. Thomas has been around for while, since 1928, presented in his book co-authored with D.S. Thomas, called *The Child in America: Behavior Problems and Programs,* published by Knopf in New York.

The concept of falsification leads into a long story of heated debate inspired by Karl Popper, the concept's source in such famous works as *The Logic of Scientific Discovery* and *Conjectures and Refutations.* I don't mean anything cosmic with the concept in terms of paradigms or the growth of science or probabilistic models or what "theory" really means. I mean it for the working scientist. I sometimes joke that I'm an "ambulatory falsification machine." It is critical for HSR that researchers, in process and in practice, *always* look for evidence that contradicts what they think they know and include those counterexamples and contradictions in their work. It is one answer to the question, "How do I know that you didn't come up with an idea and just collect material that supports what you already thought was true?" This grounded use of falsification will be a theme of chapters to come.

The famous Galileo quote comes from a book, its title translated as *The Assayer*, written in 1623. I took it off the Internet.

Einstein's quote about riding around on—or alternately riding alongside or chasing—a beam of light is a famous story found in many biographies as well as in articles and books on the concept of the "thought experiment." The "not everything that can be counted counts" line, though, might be an urban legend. Some sources say Einstein had nothing to do with it, that it actually originated in a textbook, *Informal Sociology: A Casual Introduction to Sociological Thinking*, written by William Cameron in 1963.

A like-minded colleague read this chapter and yawned at the BSS/HSR conflict I'm setting up here. Positivism died a long time ago, said he. God knows the critiques have been around a good while, going back at least to such figures as Vico and Kant in the 18th century. Now there's "anti-positivism" and "post-positivism" and "critical realism" and "social constructionism" and the beat goes on. It is a long story with an extensive literature. I had no intention of trying to cover it here. As I wrote in the preface, this book is meant to show a general reader the outlines of a different kind of human social science without dragging them through a review of everyone who's ever commented on the issue.

There's no news in a positivism critique. Instead, I wrote this book because the dominant model of human social science—among funders and human social science consumers—remains more or less BSS-like. I've reviewed grants and been on different government research funding panels where the problem I set up in this chapter is alive and well. Talks I've given on themes in this book always result in questions like, "but how do I get the supervisor/adviser/reviewer to allow HSR, the same kind of questions I was asked when I used to give methodology lectures forty years ago. I just worked on a project, in 2011, that generated spectacular creative ideas for research that the higher-ups wouldn't consider because it didn't look "scientific." As I was writing the book, I was invited to a conference at a federal agency to design multi-site research that was BSS to the core and hard to budge, though budging it was the reason the agency staff had put me on the panel. On and on go the stories, as current as last week, literally, in February of 2013, when I resigned from a project even as I uploaded this file to finish the book. BSS remains the dominant form of human social science, even as HSR continues to become more widely used.

The Dikers song is at (http://www.lyricsrequests.com/Dikers-songs-text/Dale-gas-song-lyric.html).

Chapter Two

The quotes from John Stuart Mill in this chapter come from Book III, titled "On Induction," from Volume 1 of his *A System of Logic, Ratiocinative and Inductive: Being a Connected View of the Principles of Evidence and the Methods of Scientific Investigation*, the third edition published by John Parker, London, in 1851.

Leon Festinger, with co-authors Henry W. Riecken and Stanley Schachter, wrote *When Prophecy Fails: A Social and Psycho-*

logical Study of a Modern Group that Predicted the Destruction of the World in 1956 for the University of Minnesota Press. If you do an Internet search on the concept of "cognitive dissonance" your screen will fill with an amazing variety of contemporary uses. I thought about using the more recent work on "cognitive biases" and "heuristics." A readable and recent overview by one of the founders of that field, Daniel Kahnemann, is available in his book *Thinking Fast and Slow*, published by Farrar, Straus and Giroux in 2011. In the spirit of my own book, though, I decided to stick with a classic, since one of the points I'm trying to make is that the many scattered debates around human social science are like a meteor shower that's been going on for decades.

I should say that a lot of things I write about Mill's logic and its dominance today come out of experiences as a grant reviewer for the human social science research establishment in the U.S., especially the National Institutes of Health and the National Science Foundation. I've served on official panels for periods of several years and done ad hoc reviews off and on for them and other funders for decades. As Dave Barry often writes, I am not making this up.

As of May 2012, Congress passed an amendment telling NSF to eliminate grants for political science. A professor of political science at Northwestern University, Jacqueline Stevens, wrote a heretical piece in the Sunday New York Times on June 24, 2012 where she explained why this might be happening. Most NSF funded research in the field, she wrote, "…supports research that is amenable to statistical analyses and models even though everyone knows the clean equations mask messy realities that contrived data sets and assumptions don't, and can't capture." The cracks continue to appear.

Gregory Bateson's famous double bind theory of schizophrenia can be found in an edited book of his writings, *Steps to an Ecology of Mind*, a current edition published in 2000 by the University of Chicago, though I remember borrowing the galleys from my adviser in grad school way back when. We know that schizophrenia is a lot more complicated than that now, but the "double bind" as a pattern of communication still stands, as do some of its popularizations in novels like Joseph Heller's *Catch-22*.

In this chapter I've got Mill anticipating a lot of HSR, a suspicious strategy, shaping the past to fit the present by putting modern words into a 150-year-old book. On the other hand, any fan of written or filmed stories knows that by the end you understand better what things at the beginning meant. I'll do this kind of rear-view mirror work many times in this book, since it's about how "now" comes at the end of a long path from "back then."

For instance, Mill talks about what we would call sampling issues a lot, but at times the way he talks about it foreshadows the revisionist sampling created by HSR type researchers. One famous example is the notion of "theoretical sampling" from *The Discovery of Grounded Theory* by Anselm Glaser and Barney Strauss, published in 1967 by Aldine, and considered one of the, if not the, foundational works for the qualitative research boom. Theoretical sampling introduced the heretical idea that a researcher picks the next case for a sample based on what has been learned in the research up to that point. So if you've talked to too many old people in a community you'd better talk to some young ones, or if you learned there are three factions in the town and you've only talked with people from one of them, you'd better get in touch with some of the others. This ruins the notion of random sampling, the idea that each member of a sample had to have had an equally likely chance of being chosen before a project starts.

John Lewis Gaddis wrote *The Landscape of History: How Historians Map the Past* in 2002 with Oxford University Press.

Like me and a lot of other human social scientists, he discovered nonlinear dynamic systems, or chaos and complexity theory, as it diffused out of places like the Santa Fe Institute in the late 20th century. A sea change with no end in site as I write this developed as increasing numbers of human social scientists experimented with how to integrate the formal theory's fundamentals into new ways to see our non-BSS approach to research.

The mention of Eric Hobsbawm was motivated by his book, *On History*, published by The New Press in 1997.

The idea that social science is "gappy," attributed to J.L. Mackie, I learned courtesy of the article on Mill in the online *Stanford Encyclopedia of Philosophy* by Fred Wilson, dated 2007. Mackie wrote "Mill's Methods of Induction" in the *Encyclopedia of Philosophy*, edited by P. Edwards, that Macmillan published in 1967.

I've always liked the phrase "ecological validity," I'm not sure exactly why. Maybe because it's got a snappy scientific feel to it when what it really means is, "what does that have to do with what goes on in the world?" I was surprised to learn it came from Ulric Neisser's *Cognitive Psychology*, published in 1967 by Appleton Century Crofts. I remember reading his later 1976 book, *Cognition and Reality*, published by W.H. Freeman & Co. That title suggests the concept. The web page definition of the concept that I use in this book comes from http://www.alleydog.com/glossary/definition.php?term=Ecological%20Validity.

Edward Lorenz, the meteorologist who lost track of the weather and helped found chaos theory, wrote his pioneering article in 1963, called "Deterministic nonperiodic flow," in the *Journal of Atmospheric Sciences* . The colorful "butterfly" metaphor was first used in his 1969 article "Atmospheric predictability as revealed by naturally occurring analogues," also in the *Journal of the Atmospheric Sciences* .

People ask me now and then for a good introduction to complexity theory. As I write this, there's so much material out there, in so many different fields, I'm not sure what to suggest. I still lean towards the older *Complexity: The Emerging Science at the Edge of Order and Chaos* by M. Mitchell Waldrop, published in 1992 by Touchstone. He's a physicist who somehow remained a great writer. His book tells the story of the Santa Fe Institute and the colorful cast of characters and their ideas who founded it in its first, most exciting incarnation.

The article about the marketing department at Subaru is at http://money.usnews.com/money/blogs/new-money/2009/01/05/subaru-secret-clever-marketing. If you're curious about HSR in marketing take a look at *Doing Anthropology in Consumer Research*, by Patricia Sunderland and Rita Denny, published by Left Coast Press in 2007. You can get a sense of Intel's People and Practices group at http://www.experientia.com/blog/intels-people-and-practices-research-lab/.

I've used complexity in various ways and written things about it during the illegal drug epidemic research I mention in this chapter. If you want to know more about the drug work, the best thing to do is take a look at my book, *Dope Double Agent: The Naked Emperor on Drugs*, that I put on the web with Lulubooks in 2005. The book was my farewell to the drug field and several chapters deal with specific cases we looked at. It was also the first time I experimented with the dreaded notion of "self-publishing," a term that echoes the way the nuns at St. Michael's used the term "self-abuse." I self-published that book because I was so weary of the drug field that I wanted to put the story in public as a duty to drug and country and just get it over with. Then I decided to self-publish *The Lively Science* because three book editors who were interested behaved very badly and I thought about three things: 1) Charlie Chaplin co-founded United

Artists because he was tired of dealing with producers; 2) I always sympathized with the independent truckers, a project described in this book, when they explained their career choice in terms of the country song line "take this job and shove it;" and, 3) At age 67, who am I trying to impress?

Abraham Maslow is a fascinating figure in the history of human social science who is neglected here, a prime mover in the "humanistic psychology" movement that crafted an alternative to the then dominant schools of behaviorism on the one hand and psychoanalysis on the other. His hierarchy of needs is probably known to most readers.

Hume's famous quote comes from *An Enquiry Concerning Human Understanding*, published in 1748. I cheated and just looked it up on the Internet. Given my experiences reading the original John Stuart Mill book, and the original material by Brentano and Dilthey to come in the next chapter, I'm sure there's much more to say here. I'm annoyed in retrospect at how my education consisted of brief snippets rather than fundamental ideas from the intellectual history of human social science. We had a required course freshman year in college called "The History of Western Civilization." It was the intellectual equivalent of the "Five European Countries in One Week" tour and "25 Clever Quotes to Use at Cocktail Parties."

The book about how even a massively "causally" determined disaster also takes different local shapes is an idea I took from Gregory Button's 2010 book, *Disaster Culture: Knowledge and Uncertainty in the Wake of Human and Environmental Catastrophe*, published by Left Coast Press. I actually learned about the concept in conversation with the author and cite his book because the conversation was so interesting.

Chapter Three

The *History of Philosophy* links Brentano and Dilthey on pg. 372, written by Julian Marias, published in 1967 by Dover Publications. The quote that I cite about Ortega y Gasset comes from pg. 372 of John Graham's *A Pragmatist Philosophy of Life in Ortega Y Gassett*, published in 1994 by University of Missouri Press.

Brentano quotes are taken from his *Psychology from an Empirical Standpoint*, originally published in 1874. The English language version I used first appeared in 1973, now in paperback, from Routledge. The introduction to the second edition of this version, from which I also quote, was written by Peter Simons. As with Mill I also read several items on the Internet for broader context and to ensure that the issues I was foregrounding were widely agreed to be what Brentano was about.

The issue of vague human social science jargon turned into a circus when physicist Alan Sokal published an article in 1996 titled "Transgressing the Boundaries: Towards a Transformative Hermeneutics of Quantum Gravity" in a journal called *Social Text*. At the same time that it appeared, he published an article in *Lingua Franca* saying that it was a hoax, loaded with "a pastiche of Left-wing cant, fawning references, grandiose quotations, and outright nonsense..." You can get an introduction to all the heat, and very little light, that it generated by looking up "the Sokal affair" on Wikipedia.

The Einstein quote about math and reality comes from a lecture he gave to the Prussian Academy of Science in 1921 called "Geometry and Experience."

Brentano's third person/first person distinction opens up a technical discussion worth having, but probably not here. Two jargon terms—"emic" and "etic"—have caused a lot a discussion in human social science for decades. The terms are taken from the linguist's "phonetic" and "phonemic." Sometimes they are used more or less in the sense of first person versus third person, or outsider versus insider, or researcher vs. subject. Other times they are used more or less in the sense of universal versus specific case, as I'll get to in some detail in Chapter Six. They are used in other ways as well. I'm not going to try and straighten out the mess here, but I did want to warn a reader that the mess exists in case he or she has come across the emic/etic jargon in their intellectual travels.

The quote from Daniel Dennet comes from pg. 17 of his book, *The Intentional Stance*, published by Bradford Books in 1989.

The litany of luminaries who have worked on guidelines for "making things up" when we make sense of what others are doing goes by quickly in this book. I mention them as a few of many possible examples that show how seriously this issue has been taken and how a book for professionals could be written based on this single paragraph. Here are a few references if a reader would like to begin. Wagner edited a collection of Schutz's work in 1970, *On Phenomenology and Social Relations: Selected Writings*, published by the University of Chicago Press. George Kelley's "personal construct psychology" was first published in 1955 by Norton as *The Psychology of Personal Constructs*. Weber, as some readers will know, is a central figure in the development of sociology and anthropology. His elaborate notion of social action is introduced in his essay "The Nature of Social Action," available in W. G. Runciman and E. Matthews' *Weber: Selections in Translation*, published by Cambridge University Press.

Jürgen Habermas' work is overwhelming, draws on great ideas from many sources, and has been evolving for decades. I don't know where to send a reader for a quick summary. There is a book in the "Very Short Introduction" series by Gordon Finlayson, published in 2005 as *Habermas: A Very Short Introduction*. I haven't read it myself. I can take you back in time to my old copy of *The Critical Theory of Jürgen Habermas*, written by Thomas McCarthy and published by MIT Press. My copy shows a date of 1978, ancient history I know, but it is well written and catches up with a major figure as of that date when some of his fundamental ideas took shape, including the concept of a reconstructive science that I use here. Besides—here's one valuable trick I learned early in life—if you want an overview of the work of a very complicated intellectual who wrote in a language other than English, then look for an overview written by his or her translator. McCarthy translated many of Habermas' works.

If you'd like to read more about the Austrian Schmäh concept, I used it as a centerpiece in my book about language and culture, written for a general reader and suitable for birthdays, bar mitzvahs and weddings, called *Language Shock: Understanding the Culture of Conversation,* published by Harper Paperbacks in 1996. A little dated, but of course timeless.

With the shift to Dilthey in this chapter, I rely on his classic *Introduction to the Human Sciences: An Attempt to Lay a Foundation for the Study of Society and History*, the original published in 1883. The version I used is the translation published by Wayne State University Press in 1988. Ramon J. Betanzos translated the book and wrote the introduction, which is also quoted here. As with Mill, and Brentano, the page numbers after any quotes in my book refer to this one particular volume.

Malinowski's famous quote comes from pg. 25 of one of his many classic writings, *Argonauts of the Western Pacific*, in a version published by Dutton in 1964. The book appears now in many different editions.

The quote about a "man" being like all others, some others and no others is from Henry A. Murray and Clyde Kluckhohn's 1953 book *Personality in Nature, Society and Culture*. They were part of the innovative post-World War II program at Harvard called "Social Relations" that, for a few years anyway, spanned the usual academic disciplinary fortress walls. Interesting that this is the same program where the maverick Milgram did his graduate work, a story to be told in the last chapter of this book.

If you want to see more about the TB program work, I published an article in 2000 called "Border Lessons: Linguistic "Rich Points" and Evaluative Understanding," in a special issue of *New Directions for Evaluation, How and Why Language Matters in Evaluation*, edited by Rodney K. Hopson. I got in some trouble because the project was supposed to be "evaluation research" and I was learning and experimenting with more of an organizational development approach. The difference in the two is kind of like BSS versus HSR.

The argument that "naive realism" is the fundamental problem for social psychology/social cognition is from an overview of the field written in 2005 by Gordon B. Moskowitz, *Social Cognition: Understanding Self and Others*, published by The Guilford Press.

The issue of how to combine "structure" and "agency" is common these days. Remember at the beginning of the book I talked about how behavioral/social science disciplines often chose between a focus on the individual (agency) level or the group (structure) level? Some of that came out of the origins of human social science, like Brentano arguing that psychology had its own integrity, or Durkheim later arguing for a sociological level separate from psychology. Now structure/agency is more often than not taken as part of the same science. My introduction to the synthesis came from Anthony Giddens' *Central Problems in Social*

Theory: Action, Structure, and Contradiction in Social Analysis, published back in 1979 by Macmillan. Another early entry was the work of Pierre Bourdieu with his habitus and field concepts, starting with *Outline of a Theory of Practice* in 1977, published by Cambridge University Press. I couldn't get through that one. An undergraduate told me he actually took the book out in the country and shot it. A lot of anthropologists like Sherry Ortner's article, "Theory in Anthropology Since the Sixties," published in *Comparative Studies in Society and History* in 1984, an article that gave rise to "practice theory."

I've seen and heard Hegel's famous quote about the owl spreading its wings at dusk and always liked it, along with Heidegger's quote about how you don't know what a hammer is until it breaks. I've never read either of their work in any thorough way in the original. These various sources circle around the idea that experience and analysis aren't the same thing, but that analysis based on experience that you then evaluate against future experience is where you find the right problem to investigate. The empirical versus rational distinction that drove much of Western intellectual history collapses back into the unity from whence it came, to say it in sort of a biblical way.

Ferdinand DeSaussure built his linguistics on the argument that most work with language had been historical, or "diachronic," but that language as used at a particular point in time, "synchronic," worked as a system, and when you divided language up into historical chunks for comparison you missed that. A new version of his *Course in General Linguistics*, listed with W. Baskin as co-author, was published by Columbia University in 2011. The original, based on notes his students took in his course—hence the title—came out in 1916. He's considered outdated now, having been deconstructed by Derrida and blurred with language variation by many. An overview of DeSaussure, and another figure to come in this book, Charles Peirce, is available in Daniel Chandler's 2002 book *Semiotics: The Basics,* published by Routledge and also on the web.

The movie *Rashomon* is famous and available on Netflix and probably any other rental source a reader has access to. Karl Heider, a founder of visual anthropology, wrote about it in "The Rashomon Effect: When Ethnographers Disagree," in the *American Anthropologist* in 1988.

Dilthey's argument about the nature of reality, in the translated original, is available in *Wilhelm Dilthey: Selected Works, Volume II: Understanding the Human World*, edited by Rudolf A. Makkreel and Frithjof Rodi, published in 2012 by Princeton, the original in 1890. I relied on descriptions of the work by the translator of his *Introduction to the Human Sciences.*

The famous story of Johnson kicking the rock, one I heard and never forgot because it sounds like something I'd do, comes from James Boswell's *Life of Johnson*, originally published in 1791.

Chapter Four

Toulmin's comments on writing come from an interview transcript on the web at http://www.scribd.com/doc/95728215/An-interview-with-philosopher-Stephen-Toulmin. His most famous book, *The Uses of Argument,* was originally published in 1958 by Cambridge. A later book, *Return to Reason*, published in 2001 by Harvard, generalizes his ideas well beyond questions of human social science. Peter Nosbers and I, Peter being a student who worked with me in Vienna, used Toulmin to look at "argumentation" in the discourse literature. We published in both German and English, the English version appearing in a journal called *Semiotica* in 1993, "Argumentation and the Distance to the Data." In this book, I mention Toulmin's later work with physicians. It appears, among other places, in a chapter in *Science, Technology and the Art of Medicine*, edited by Delkeskamp-Hayes and Cutler in 1993, titled "Knowledge and Art in the Practice of Medicine."

There are dozens of examples of Toulmin's diagram on the Internet. The one I used here comes from http://www-rohan.sdsu.edu/~digger/305/toulmin_model.htm.

Owen Murdoch and I invented the "quanltative" word in a report called "Investigating Recent Trends in Heroin Use in Baltimore City: A Pilot 'Quanltative' Research Project". It was printed by the Center for Substance Abuse Research at the University of Maryland in 1994. To my surprise as I prepared these chapter notes, it is listed on several web sites, though I couldn't find one that offers an actual copy and mine got lost in the move from D.C. to the Southwest.

The business of self-reference is a high altitude tightrope in human social science, but an inevitable one that a researcher has to walk sooner or later. The research can't be just about them, nor can it be just about you. It is about both of you at the same time, hence the use of the word "intersubjective." A popular book that introduces the self-reference theme in a mathematical sense is Hofstadter's *Gödel, Escher, Bach: An Eternal Golden Braid*, originally published in 1979 by Basic Books and reissued in a 20th Anniversary edition in 1999.

The Hawthorne effect, the observation that the way human social science is done has something to do with its results, is discussed in several places through the years and across the disciplines, almost always as a problem to be solved rather than a simple fact about human social research that has to be incorporated into the science.

The event is also famous in applied anthropology as an early moment when anthropologists did something besides head off to isolated non-U.S.—or American Indian—settings to do their work.

Elliot Mishler's original version of shifting from BSS to HSR is described in his book, *Research Interviewing: Context and Narrative*, published by Harvard in 1986. We met when he attended the meetings of GURT, not the most elegant acronym, the Georgetown University Round Table on Languages and Linguistics, in the 1980s. I always think of him as a kindred spirit in the sense of how hard it is to go into a student/learning role after you're established in some academic/human social science track. I wish I could have done it as well as he did.

In anthropology, the 1986 publication of *Writing Culture: The Poetics and Politics of Ethnography*, by James Clifford and George Marcus by the University of California Press, it was a big deal. It meant to liberate us all, in its own opaque academic way, from opaque academic writing. Personally I appreciated the book and think it had a powerful and positive effect on anthropology . Over in sociology, John Van Maanen wrote *Tales of the Field: On Writing Ethnography*, in 1988 with the University of Chicago. The former book was recently issued in a 25th anniversary edition and the latter, a bit earlier, in a 20th anniversary version. John's book makes the same general point and is a lot more fun to read.

Chapter Five

"Nonmonotonic" has a nice rhythm to it. I cite David Markinson's *Bridges from Classical to Nonmonotonic Logic*, published in 2005 by College Publications. I took the original Peirce quote about abduction used in this book from a paper by Michael Hoffman, an artificial intelligence researcher, the quote originally from Peirce's collected papers, published in 1906, issued by Harvard University Press in 1932, edited by Charles Hartshorne and Paul Weiss. The comparison of Peirce and Sherlock Holmes is by Thomas A. Sebeok and D. J. Umiker-Sebeok, *'You Know My Method:' A Juxtaposition of Charles S. Peirce and Sherlock Holmes*, published in 1980 by Gaslight Publications.

The research with independent truckers, more accurately, owner-operators, came out in a 1986 book called *Independents Declared: The Dilemmas of Independent Trucking,* published by Smithsonian Press. It had a sad life. Cornell University Press wanted it but then their academic board dumped it because it wasn't academic enough. Smithsonian published it but then wouldn't sell it at a bookstore discount so it never appeared on the shelves. Then Smithsonian quit printing it. Oh well, Studs Terkel and the owner-operators and my Teamster cousin Don liked it.

As I mention in this book, I use the Peirce quote that I do because it lends itself to HSR, namely, to the importance of noticing the unexpected and imagining what might explain it. I mentioned in the book that there are more closed versions of abduction, for example the way it is often used in artificial intelligence. Say we've got P → Q, and you know P, therefore you infer Q. That is classic deduction. Or say we've got P occurring with Q, so we infer P → Q. That is classic induction. So if we have P → Q and Q, we can then infer P? That is a mortal sin, in classical logic. Abduction allows the sin back in. But this example of abduction is much more constrained by propositional form than the way that I'm using it here. Peirce used both—and other—versions at different times as well.

I mention George Herbert Mead as another foundational figure of HSR who imported German ideas into the U.S. One classic reference for him is the 1934 book *Mind Self and Society*, published by the University of Chicago. He was part of the development of the Chicago school of sociology, mentioned in this book, and the beginning of "symbolic interactionism," an HSR stream within the dominant BSS tradition that came to characterize most of American sociology.

Chapter Six

The characteristics of human language that are described in this chapter, like duality of patterning and arbitrariness and productivity, come from an old article by Charles Hockett, one reference being a chapter he co-authored with Stuart Altmann in 1968 in a book edited by the same Thomas Sebeok who wrote about Peirce and Sherlock Holmes, this one called *Animal Communication: Techniques of Study and Results of Research*, published by Indiana University.

The evolution of language is such a hot topic these days, reflected in so many academic and popular publications, that I hesitate to recommend anything. It mixes in with primate communication, child development, all the hyphenated human social science/biology mixes, and even Alan Alda's PBS series, "The Human Spark." The book on my shelf awaiting attention right now is Michael Tomasello's *Origins of Human Communication*, published in 2008 by MIT. In this section I draw on Philip Lieberman, *Uniquely Human: The Evolution of Speech, Thought and Selfless Behavior*, Harvard 1991; Charles Hockett, "The Origin of Speech" in *The Scientific Ameri*can in 1960; Merlin Donald, *Origins of the Modern Mind: Three Stages in the Evolution of Culture and Cognition*, Harvard 1993, and Robbins Burling, *The Talking Ape: How Language Evolved*, Oxford 2007.

The story I tell about Herbert Huncke, the old-time New York heroin addict, turned into a chapter in a book with Jerry Hobbs, an artificial intelligence researcher. We called it "How to Grow Schemas out of Interviews," and it was published in 1985 in *Directions in Cognitive Anthropology* that Jan Dougherty edited for the University of Illinois. Imagine my surprise when I wandered one day into City Lights bookstore in San Francisco and looked at a copy of *The Beat Journey,* edited by Arthur and Kit Knight, published in 1978. There was the same interview about learning burglary that Jerry and I had used in the chapter. And fair enough, I'd left Huncke with copies of the transcripts so he could do something with them as well. In this book, I make a joke about how Huncke didn't acknowledge my help at editing the transcripts for him. It is a joke. My other joke is, I once wrote that I was going to file a complaint with the ethics committee of the American Anthropological Association, saying that a subject had ripped me off. The joke was based on their assumption was that the only possible case would be exactly the opposite.

Laura Bohannon's article, "Shakespeare in the Bush," was originally published in *Nature* in 1966. It is easy to find a full reprint on the web. I used http://www.naturalhistorymag.com/ editors_pick/1966_08-09_pick.html.The discussion of translation in this chapter draws from work I did recently, summarized in an article called "Making Sense of One Other for Another: Ethnography as Translation." It appeared in 2011 in a journal called *Language and Communication*. I quote from a few sources that I used in that article. The Ifaluk emotion examples come from Catherine Lutz's 1988 book, *Unnatural Emotions: Everyday Sentiments on a Micronesian Atoll,* published by the University of Chicago. A book that turned translation in the direction of many of the issues discussed here is Susan Bassnet-Maguire's *Notes on*

Translation Studies, published in 1980 by Methuen. I also use a quote from Paula Rubel and Abe Rossman's introduction to their 2003 edited book, *Translating Cultures: Perspectives on Translation and Anthropology*, published by Berg.

If you'd like a good recent and readable book about translation, take a look at *Is That a Fish in Your Ear? Translation and the Meaning of Everything* by David Bellos, published by Faber and Faber in 2012.

Donald Brown's book *Human Universals* was published in 1991 by McGraw-Hill. A more recent update is in an article he wrote for *Daedalus* in 2004 called "Human Universals, Human Nature & Human Culture." The hi-tech video where he briefly summarizes his argument is at http://www.pangeaday.org/film-Detail.php?id=18.

Joseph Henrich, along with his co-authors Steven J. Heine and Ara Norenzayan, caused a stir with their 2010 article "The Weirdest People in the World," published in *Behavioral and Brain Sciences*. It appeared with numerous commentaries and an Internet search will bring up all sorts of discussions and debates. It establishes what anthropologists have complained about for decades. You can never assume that human social science in one society generalizes to all of humanity, or even to all of that society for that matter.

Robert Redfield's 1948 article, "The Art of Social Science," was published in The *American Journal of Sociology*.

Chapter Seven

Thomas Blass's book, *The Man Who Shocked the World: The Life and Legacy of Stanley Milgram*, came out in 2004 with Basic Books. As I describe in this chapter, I had already decided that

The Lively Science had to end by challenging my HSR ranting and raving with a powerful and massively important example of BSS. I considered using the recent work on cognitive biases that led to behavioral economics as something that would catch a reader's attention, also well summarized in Daniel Kahnemann's recent book, mentioned in the notes for the first chapter. But I've always been partial to those classic social psychology experiments that still make the news. And with Milgram there's a biographical link because of my long history with Austria and the resurgence of World War II issues that commenced in that country in earnest in the 1980s.

As the chapter shifts, with Milgram's story as the pivot, into the general issue of the larger context of human social science, or any other project for that matter, I tell a few more stories from the U.S. drug field and its insane "war on drugs" policy of more than forty years. As I mentioned earlier, I did a farewell book called *Dope Double Agent: The Naked Emperor on Drugs* in 2005 that contains plenty of material to support what I say.

Jürgen Habermas' concept of Erkentnisinteresse, translated into English, is in fact the title of his book *Knowledge and Human Interests,* published by Beacon Press in 1972. It is only one stage in his long journey and it is about more than the use of just that concept. The famous Frankfurt school was one of his early stops on that journey, though in my opinion the description that you often hear—that he carries on that tradition—oversimplifies his complicated thinking and its evolution over the decades. I often hear arguments that dismiss Habermas because of his work on "universal pragmatics," where he imagined that consensus could always be reached among different perspectives if we just straightened out communication in a universal way. Naïve, say colleagues, and I couldn't agree more. But his ideas that I use here, like rational reconstruction and knowledge and human interests, come from different arguments he made and don't depend on whether we can "just all get along," as Rodney King hoped for.

The quotes about Edith Stein in my book are from a web essay by Frances Horner at http://www.carmelstream.com/?p=35. Among other web resources, I also benefited from Marianne Sawicki's essay, "Personal Connections: The Phenomenology of Edith Stein," at http://www.library.nd.edu/colldev/subject_home_pages/catholic/personal_connections.shtml. Several books about Stein are now available, including a translation of her own *On the Problem of Empathy*, in the series The Collected Works of Edith Stein, translated by Waltraut Stein and published in 1989 by ICS publications.

At the end of the book I mention HSR work by colleagues in Speech Communication and Political Science and cite examples in the text. I also mention Ann Cunliffe. A recent readable book that shows HSR in action in business is her *A Very Short, Fairly Interesting and Reasonably Cheap Book about Management*, published by Sage in 2009, in the series of the same name. I mention Peter Drucker in passing, another Austrian immigrant to the U.S. by the way. I had no particular reference to his many writings in mind, just the sense of him as a person who thought of business in broad and deep historical contexts.

Most readers will recognize the notion of a "paradigm shift" as described by Thomas Kuhn in his *The Structure of Scientific Revolutions*, now in its 1996 third edition. I wish I had a nickel for every time a human social scientist, BSS or HSR, announced that they had just produced a new paradigm. But, in Kuhn's sense of a marked generational shift in how to think about human social science, as reflected in my own lifetime from the mid-1960s until the present, that's what it looks like is happening with HSR.

The purpose of *The Lively Science* is to highlight some important features of the shift by learning from past efforts that set the stage. No shift before it's time.

Finally, most any named topic or intellectual figure in this book can be easily found in more elaborate form with an Internet search, should a reader be interested. I often tell younger students and colleagues, I am deeply grateful that I got out of graduate school long before the invention of the Internet. All we had were card catalogues and narrow subdisciplines which limited the material that we had to cover. Add to that the fact that most any interesting intellectual problem these days sits at the center of *no* traditional discipline, and I can't figure out how the contemporary graduate student finds a groove and a faculty committee to support it. It would make a fascinating HSR study and might even teach us something useful about how to change the university.

CPSIA information can be obtained at www.ICGtesting.com
Printed in the USA
BVOW03s0004060913

330302BV00008B/530/P